JSCRIPT AND WBEMSCRIPTING ASYNC

Working with ExecNotificationQueryAsync and __InstanceModificationEvent

Richard Thomas Edwards

CONTENTS

Getting Started..8

ASP Reports 11

    Begin Code 11

    Horizontal No Additional Tags...12

    Horizontal Using A Button..12

    Horizontal Using A ComboBox 12

    Horizontal Using A Div...13

    Horizontal Using A Link..13

    Horizontal Using A ListBox 14

    Horizontal Using A Span..14

    Horizontal Using A Textarea 15

    Horizontal Using A TextBox 15

    Vertical No Additional Controls..16

    Vertical Using A Button...16

    Vertical Using A ComboBox 17

    Vertical Using A Div..17

    Vertical Using A Link..17

    Vertical Using A ListBox..18

Vertical Using A Span 18

Vertical Using A Textarea 19

Vertical Using A TextBox 19

End Code 20

ASP Tables 21

Begin Code 21

function Write_The_Code() 21

Horizontal No Additional Tags 22

Horizontal Using A Button 22

Horizontal Using A ComboBox 22

Horizontal Using A Div 23

Horizontal Using A Link 23

Horizontal Using A ListBox 24

Horizontal Using A Span 24

Horizontal Using A Textarea 25

Horizontal Using A TextBox 25

Vertical No Additional Controls 26

Vertical Using A Button 26

Vertical Using A ComboBox 26

Vertical Using A Div 27

Vertical Using A Link 27

Vertical Using A ListBox 28

Vertical Using A Span 28

Vertical Using A Textarea 29

Vertical Using A TextBox 29

End Code 30

ASPX Reports 31

Begin Code 31

Horizontal No Additional Tags 32

Horizontal Using A Button 32

Horizontal Using A ComboBox 33

Horizontal Using A Div 33

Horizontal Using A Link 33

Horizontal Using A ListBox 34

Horizontal Using A Span 34

Horizontal Using A Textarea 35

Horizontal Using A TextBox...35

Vertical No Additional Controls 36

Vertical Using A Button 36

Vertical Using A ComboBox 37

Vertical Using A Div..37

Vertical Using A Link 38

Vertical Using A ListBox 38

Vertical Using A Span..38

Vertical Using A Textarea 39

Vertical Using A TextBox...39

End Code 40

ASPX TABLES..41

Begin Code...41

Horizontal No Additional Tags 42

Horizontal Using A Button 42

Horizontal Using A ComboBox 42

Horizontal Using A Div 43

Horizontal Using A Link 43

Horizontal Using A ListBox..44

Horizontal Using A Span 44

Horizontal Using A Textarea...45

Horizontal Using A TextBox...45

Vertical No Additional Controls...46

Vertical Using A Button 46

Vertical Using A ComboBox 46

Vertical Using A Div 47

Vertical Using A Link 47

Vertical Using A ListBox..48

Vertical Using A Span 48

Vertical Using A Textarea...49

Vertical Using A TextBox..49

End Code 50

HTA REPORTS..51

Begin Code 51

Horizontal No Additional Tags 51

Horizontal Using A Button 52

Horizontal Using A ComboBox..52

Horizontal Using A Div 53

Horizontal Using A Link 53

Horizontal Using A ListBox...54

Horizontal Using A Span 54

Horizontal Using A Textarea..54

Horizontal Using A TextBox..55

Vertical No Additional Controls 55

Vertical Using A Button 56

Vertical Using A ComboBox...56

Vertical Using A Div 57

Vertical Using A Link 57

Vertical Using A ListBox..57

Vertical Using A Span 58

Vertical Using A Textarea...58

Vertical Using A TextBox..59

End Code 59

HTA TABLES 60

Begin Code 60

Horizontal No Additional Tags 61

Horizontal Using A Button 61

Horizontal Using A ComboBox..61

Horizontal Using A Div...62

Horizontal Using A Link...62

Horizontal Using A ListBox...63

Horizontal Using A Span...63

Horizontal Using A Textarea...63

Horizontal Using A TextBox..64

Vertical No Additional Controls..64

Vertical Using A Button..65

Vertical Using A ComboBox..65

Vertical Using A Div...66

Vertical Using A Link...66

Vertical Using A ListBox...67

Vertical Using A Span..67

Vertical Using A Textarea...67

Vertical Using A TextBox..68

End Code...68

HTML REPORTS 69

Begin Code..69

Horizontal No Additional Tags...69

Horizontal Using A Button..70

Horizontal Using A ComboBox 70

Horizontal Using A Div...71

Horizontal Using A Link..71

Horizontal Using A ListBox...71

Horizontal Using A Span 72

Horizontal Using A Textarea...72

Horizontal Using A TextBox..73

Vertical No Additional Controls 73

Vertical Using A Button 74

Vertical Using A ComboBox..74

Vertical Using A Div 75

Vertical Using A Link 75

Vertical Using A ListBox 75

Vertical Using A Span 76

Vertical Using A Textarea 76

Vertical Using A TextBox 77

End Code 77

HTML TABLES 78

Begin Code 78

Horizontal No Additional Tags 78

Horizontal Using A Button 79

Horizontal Using A ComboBox 79

Horizontal Using A Div..80

Horizontal Using A Link...80

Horizontal Using A ListBox...80

Horizontal Using A Span 81

Horizontal Using A Textarea 81

Horizontal Using A TextBox..82

Vertical No Additional Controls 82

Vertical Using A Button 83

Vertical Using A ComboBox..83

Vertical Using A Div 83

Vertical Using A Link..84

Vertical Using A ListBox..84

Vertical Using A Span 85

Vertical Using A Textarea 85

Vertical Using A TextBox...85

End Code 86

Stylesheets 87

NONE 87

BLACK AND WHITE TEXT 88

COLORED TEXT...91

OSCILLATING ROW COLORS 94

GHOST DECORATED 97

3D 100

SHADOW BOX 106

Getting Started

THIS IS A BOOK OF CODE. It includes ASP, ASPX, HTA and HTML Reports and tables being generated by WbemScripting and Get to power them.

No book is perfect and I'm sure you will find the usual small coding issues a book of this size is naturally going to have.

Aside from that, both table and report type views are part of the source code and each of those use an assortment of controls. The core code is below:

```
var doneonce = new String;
doneonce="false";

var x=0;
var y=0;
var z=0;
var names = new Array();
var values = new Array();
var va = new Array();

function GetValue(Name, obj)
{
    var tempstr = new String;
    var tempstr1 = new String;
    var tName = new String;
    tempstr1 = obj.GetObjectText_(0);
```

```javascript
    var re = /"/g;
    tempstr1 = tempstr1.replace(re , "");
    var pos;
    tName = "\t" + Name + " = ";
    pos = tempstr1.indexOf(tName);
    if (pos > -1)
    {
      pos = pos + tName.length;
      tempstr = tempstr1.substr(pos, tempstr1.length);
      pos = tempstr.indexOf(";");
      tempstr = tempstr.substr(0, pos);
      tempstr = tempstr.replace("{", "");
      tempstr = tempstr.replace("}", "");
      if (tempstr.length > 13)
      {
        if (obj.Properties_(Name).CIMType == 101)
        {
          tempstr = tempstr.substr(4, 2) + "/"  + tempstr.substr(6, 2) + "/" +
tempstr.substr(0, 3) + " " + tempstr.substr(8, 2) + ":" + tempstr.substr(10, 2) + ":" +
tempstr.substr(12, 2);
        }
      }
      return tempstr;
    }
    else
    {
      return "";
    }
  }
  function sink_OnObjectReady(objWbemObject, objWbemAsyncContext)
  {
    var obj = objWbemObject.TargetInstance;
    var propset = obj.properties_;
    var propEnum = new Enumerator(propset);
    for(;!propEnum.atEnd();propEnum.moveNext())
    {
      var prop = propEnum.item();
      if (doneonce == "false")
      {
        names[x] = prop.Name;
```

```
          va[x] = GetValue(prop.Name, obj);
        }
        else
        {
          va[x] = GetValue(prop.Name, obj);
        }
        x++;
      }
      doneonce = true;
      values[y] = va
      x = 0;
     if y ==4)
    {
        Write_The_Code();
        Sink.Cancel();
    }
      y++;
    }

    var v=0;

    var mysink = WScript.CreateObject("WbemScripting.SWbemSink", "sink_");
    var l = new ActiveXObject("WbemScripting.SWbemLocator");
    var svc = l.ConnectServer(".", "root\\cimv2",,, "MS-0409");
    svc.ExecNotificationQueryAsync(mysink, "Select * from
___InstanceModificationEvent WITHIN 1 where TargetInstance ISA
'Win32_Process'");
```

Begin Code

```
function Write_The_Code()
{
    var ws = new ActiveXObject("WScript.Shell");
    var filename = ws.CurrentDirectory + "\\Win32_Process.asp";
    var fso = new ActiveXObject("Scripting.FileSystemObject");
    var txtstream = fso.OpenTextFile(filename, 2, true, -2);
    txtstream.writeline("<html xmlns=\"http://www.w3.org/1999/xhtml\">");
    txtstream.WriteLine("<head>");
    txtstream.WriteLine("<title>Win32_Process</title>");
    txtstream.WriteLine("</head>");
    txtstream.WriteLine("<body>");
    txtstream.WriteLine("<%");
    txtstream.WriteLine("Response.Write(\"<table cellpadding=2 cellspacing=2>\" &
vbcrlf)");
    txtstream.WriteLine("Response.Write(\"<tr>\" & vbcrlf)");
    for(var c = 0;c < names.length;c++)
    {
        txtstream.WriteLine("Response.Write(\"<th           style='color:darkred;font-
size:10px;font-family:Cambria, serif;' align='left' nowrap>" + names[c] + "</th>\"
& vbcrlf)");
    }
    txtstream.WriteLine("Response.Write(\"</tr>\" & vbcrlf)");
```

Horizontal No Additional Tags

```
for(var d = 0;d < values.length;d++)
{
    txtstream.WriteLine("Response.Write(\"<tr>\" & vbcrlf)");
    va = values[d];
    for(var c = 0;c < names.length;c++)
    {
        txtstream.WriteLine("Response.Write(\"<td                style='color:navy;font-
size:10px;font-family:Cambria, serif;' align='left' nowrap>" + va[c] + "</td>\" &
vbcrlf)");
    }
    txtstream.WriteLine("Response.Write(\"</tr>\" & vbcrlf)");
}
```

Horizontal Using A Button

```
for(var d = 0;d < values.length;d++)
{
    txtstream.WriteLine("Response.Write(\"<tr>\" & vbcrlf)");
    va = values[d];
    for(var c = 0;c < names.length;c++)
    {
        txtstream.WriteLine("Response.Write(\"<td                style='color:navy;font-
size:10px;font-family:Cambria, serif;' align='left' nowrap><input Type= button
value=\"\" + va[c] + \"\"></input></td>\" & vbcrlf)");
    }
    txtstream.WriteLine("Response.Write(\"</tr>\" & vbcrlf)");
}
```

Horizontal Using A ComboBox

```
for(var d = 0;d < values.length;d++)
{
    txtstream.WriteLine("Response.Write(\"<tr>\" & vbcrlf)");
```

```
    va = values[d];
    for(var c = 0;c < names.length;c++)
    {
        txtstream.WriteLine("Response.Write(\"<td style='font-family:Calibri, Sans-
Serif;font-size: 12px;color:navy;' align='left' nowrap='true'><select><option value =
'" + va[c] + "'>" + va[c] + "</option></select></td>\" + vbcrlf)");
    }
    txtstream.WriteLine("Response.Write(\"</tr>\" & vbcrlf)");
}
```

Horizontal Using A Div

```
for(var d = 0;d < values.length;d++)
{
        txtstream.WriteLine("Response.Write(\"<tr>\" & vbcrlf)");
        va = values[d];
        for(var c = 0;c < names.length;c++)
        {

            txtstream.WriteLine("Response.Write(\"<td        style='color:navy;font-
size:10px;font-family:Cambria,  serif;'  align='left'  nowrap><div>" + va[c] +
"</div></td>\" & vbcrlf)");

    }
    txtstream.WriteLine("Response.Write(\"</tr>\" & vbcrlf)");
}
```

Horizontal Using A Link

```
for(var d = 0;d < values.length;d++)
{
    txtstream.WriteLine("Response.Write(\"<tr>\" & vbcrlf)");
    va = values[d];
    for(var c = 0;c < names.length;c++)
    {
```

```
        txtstream.WriteLine("Response.Write(\"<td style='font-family:Calibri, Sans-
Serif;font-size: 12px;color:navy;' align='left' nowrap='true'><a href='" + va[c] +
"'>" + va[c] + "</a></td>\" + vbcrlf)");
    }
    txtstream.WriteLine("Response.Write(\"</tr>\" & vbcrlf)");
  }
```

Horizontal Using A ListBox

```
  for(var d = 0;d < values.length;d++

  {

    txtstream.WriteLine("Response.Write(\"<tr>\" & vbcrlf)");

    va = values[d];
    for(var c = 0;c < names.length;c++)
    {
        txtstream.WriteLine("Response.Write(\"<td style='font-family:Calibri, Sans-
Serif;font-size:      12px;color:navy;'      align='left'      nowrap='true'><select
multiple><option value = '" + va[c] + "'>" + va[c] + "</option></select></td>\" +
vbcrlf)");
    }
    txtstream.WriteLine("Response.Write(\"</tr>\" & vbcrlf)");
  }
```

Horizontal Using A Span

```
  for(var d = 0;d < values.length;d++

  {

    txtstream.WriteLine("Response.Write(\"<tr>\" & vbcrlf)");

    va = values[d];
    for(var c = 0;c < names.length;c++)
    {
        txtstream.WriteLine("Response.Write(\"<td           style='color:navy;font-
size:10px;font-family:Cambria, serif;' align='left' nowrap><span>" + va[c] +
"</span></td>\" & vbcrlf)");
    }
    txtstream.WriteLine("Response.Write(\"</tr>\" & vbcrlf)");
```

```
}
```

Horizontal Using A Textarea

```
for(var d = 0;d < values.length;d++

{

   txtstream.WriteLine("Response.Write(\"<tr>\" & vbcrlf)");

   va = values[d];
   for(var c = 0;c < names.length;c++)
   {
       txtstream.WriteLine("Response.Write(\"<td          style='color:navy;font-
size:10px;font-family:Cambria, serif;' align='left' nowrap><textarea>" + va[c] +
"</textarea></td>\" & vbcrlf)");
   }
   txtstream.WriteLine("Response.Write(\"</tr>\" & vbcrlf)");
}
```

Horizontal Using A TextBox

```
for(var d = 0;d < values.length;d++

{

   txtstream.WriteLine("Response.Write(\"<tr>\" & vbcrlf)");

   va = values[d];
   for(var c = 0;c < names.length;c++)
   {
       txtstream.WriteLine("Response.Write(\"<td          style='color:navy;font-
size:10px;font-family:Cambria,   serif;'   align='left'   nowrap><input   Type=text
value=\"\" + va[c] + \"\"></input></td>\" & vbcrlf)");

   }
   txtstream.WriteLine("Response.Write(\"</tr>\" & vbcrlf)");
}
```

Vertical No Additional Controls

```
for(var c = 0;c < names.length;c++)
{
    txtstream.WriteLine("Response.Write(\"<tr><th        style='color:darkred;font-
size:10px;font-family:Cambria, serif;' align='left' nowrap>" + names[c] + "</th>\"
& vbcrlf)");
    for(var d = 0;d < values.length;d++)
    {
      va = values[d];
        txtstream.WriteLine("Response.Write(\"<td              style='color:navy;font-
size:10px;font-family:Cambria, serif;' align='left' nowrap>" + va[c] + "</td>\" &
vbcrlf)");
    }
    txtstream.WriteLine("Response.Write(\"</tr>\" & vbcrlf)");
}
```

Vertical Using A Button

```
for(var c = 0;c < names.length;c++)
{
    txtstream.WriteLine("Response.Write(\"<tr><th        style='color:darkred;font-
size:10px;font-family:Cambria, serif;' align='left' nowrap>" + names[c] + "</th>\"
& vbcrlf)");
    for(var d = 0;d < values.length;d++)
    {
      va = values[d];
        txtstream.WriteLine("Response.Write(\"<td              style='color:navy;font-
size:10px;font-family:Cambria, serif;' align='left' nowrap><input Type= button
value=\"\" + va[c] + \"\"></input></td>\" & vbcrlf)");
    }
    txtstream.WriteLine("Response.Write(\"</tr>\" & vbcrlf)");
}
```

Vertical Using A ComboBox

```
for(var c = 0;c < names.length;c++)
{
    txtstream.WriteLine("Response.Write(\"<tr><th        style='color:darkred;font-
size:10px;font-family:Cambria, serif;' align='left' nowrap>" + names[c] + "</th>\"
& vbcrlf)");
    for(var d = 0;d < values.length;d++)
    {
        va = values[d];
        txtstream.WriteLine("Response.Write(\"<td style='font-family:Calibri, Sans-
Serif;font-size: 12px;color:navy;' align='left' nowrap='true'><select><option value =
'" + va[c] + "'>" + va[c] + "</option></select></td>\" + vbcrlf)");
    }
    txtstream.WriteLine("Response.Write(\"</tr>\" & vbcrlf)");
}
```

Vertical Using A Div

```
for(var c = 0;c < names.length;c++)
{
    txtstream.WriteLine("Response.Write(\"<tr><th        style='color:darkred;font-
size:10px;font-family:Cambria, serif;' align='left' nowrap>" + names[c] + "</th>\"
& vbcrlf)");
    for(var d = 0;d < values.length;d++)
    {
        va = values[d];
        txtstream.WriteLine("Response.Write(\"<td              style='color:navy;font-
size:10px;font-family:Cambria,  serif;'  align='left'  nowrap><div>"  +  va[c]  +
"</div></td>\" & vbcrlf)");
    }
    txtstream.WriteLine("Response.Write(\"</tr>\" & vbcrlf)")
}
```

Vertical Using A Link

```
for(var c = 0;c < names.length;c++)
```

```
    {
        txtstream.WriteLine("Response.Write(\"<tr><th        style='color:darkred;font-
size:10px;font-family:Cambria, serif;' align='left' nowrap>" + names[c] + "</th>\"
& vbcrlf)");
        for(var d = 0;d < values.length;d++)
        {
            va = values[d];
            txtstream.WriteLine("Response.Write(\"<td style='font-family:Calibri, Sans-
Serif;font-size: 12px;color:navy;' align='left' nowrap='true'><a href='" + va[c] +
"'>" + va[c] + "</a></td>\" + vbcrlf)");
        }
        txtstream.WriteLine("Response.Write(\"</tr>\" & vbcrlf)");
    }
```

Vertical Using A ListBox

```
    for(var c = 0;c < names.length;c++)
    {
        txtstream.WriteLine("Response.Write(\"<tr><th        style='color:darkred;font-
size:10px;font-family:Cambria, serif;' align='left' nowrap>" + names[c] + "</th>\"
& vbcrlf)");
        for(var d = 0;d < values.length;d++)
        {
            va = values[d];
            txtstream.WriteLine("Response.Write(\"<td style='font-family:Calibri, Sans-
Serif;font-size:    12px;color:navy;'     align='left'     nowrap='true'><select
multiple><option value = '" + va[c] + "'>" + va[c] + "</option></select></td>\" +
vbcrlf)");
        }
        txtstream.WriteLine("Response.Write(\"</tr>\" & vbcrlf)");
    }
```

Vertical Using A Span

```
    for(var c = 0;c < names.length;c++)
    {
        txtstream.WriteLine("Response.Write(\"<tr><th        style='color:darkred;font-
size:10px;font-family:Cambria, serif;' align='left' nowrap>" + names[c] + "</th>\"
& vbcrlf)");
        for(var d = 0;d < values.length;d++)
```

```
    {
       va = values[d];
       txtstream.WriteLine("Response.Write(\"<td           style='color:navy;font-
size:10px;font-family:Cambria,  serif;'  align='left'  nowrap><span>" + va[c] +
"</span></td>\" & vbcrlf)");
    }
    txtstream.WriteLine("Response.Write(\"</tr>\" & vbcrlf)");
}
```

Vertical Using A Textarea

```
for(var c = 0;c < names.length;c++)
{
    txtstream.WriteLine("Response.Write(\"<tr><th        style='color:darkred;font-
size:10px;font-family:Cambria, serif;' align='left' nowrap>" + names[c] + "</th>\"
& vbcrlf)");
    for(var d = 0;d < values.length;d++)
    {
       va = values[d];
       txtstream.WriteLine("Response.Write(\"<td           style='color:navy;font-
size:10px;font-family:Cambria,  serif;'  align='left'  nowrap><textarea>" + va[c] +
"</textarea></td>\" & vbcrlf)");
    }
    txtstream.WriteLine("Response.Write(\"</tr>\" & vbcrlf)");
}
```

Vertical Using A TextBox

```
for(var c = 0;c < names.length;c++)
{
    txtstream.WriteLine("Response.Write(\"<tr><th        style='color:darkred;font-
size:10px;font-family:Cambria, serif;' align='left' nowrap>" + names[c] + "</th>\"
& vbcrlf)");
    for(var d = 0;d < values.length;d++)
    {
       va = values[d];
       txtstream.WriteLine("Response.Write(\"<td           style='color:navy;font-
size:10px;font-family:Cambria,   serif;'   align='left'   nowrap><input   Type=text
value=\"\" + va[c] + \"\"></input></td>\" & vbcrlf)");
```

```
        }
        txtstream.WriteLine("Response.Write(\"</tr>\" & vbcrlf)");
    }
```

End Code

```
    txtstream.WriteLine("Response.Write(\"</table>\" & vbcrlf)");
    txtstream.WriteLine("%>");
    txtstream.WriteLine("</body>");
    txtstream.WriteLine("</html>");
    txtstream.Close();

}
```

ASP Tables

Begin Code

function Write_The_Code()

```
{
    var ws = new ActiveXObject("WScript.Shell");
    var filename = ws.CurrentDirectory + "\\Win32_Process.asp";
    var fso = new ActiveXObject("Scripting.FileSystemObject");
    var txtstream = fso.OpenTextFile(filename, 2, true, -2);
    txtstream.writeline("<html xmlns=\"http://www.w3.org/1999/xhtml\">");
    txtstream.WriteLine("<head>");
    txtstream.WriteLine("<title>Win32_Process</title>");
    txtstream.WriteLine("</head>");
    txtstream.WriteLine("<body>");
    txtstream.WriteLine("<%");
    txtstream.WriteLine("Response.Write(\"<table     Border=1     cellpadding=2
cellspacing=2>\" & vbcrlf)");
    txtstream.WriteLine("Response.Write(\"<tr>\" & vbcrlf)");
    for(var c = 0;c < names.length;c++)
    {
        txtstream.WriteLine("Response.Write(\"<th          style='color:darkred;font-
size:10px;font-family:Cambria, serif;' align='left' nowrap>" + names[c] + "</th>\"
& vbcrlf)");
    }
    txtstream.WriteLine("Response.Write(\"</tr>\" & vbcrlf)");
```

Horizontal No Additional Tags

```
for(var d = 0;d < values.length;d++)
{
    txtstream.WriteLine("Response.Write(\"<tr>\" & vbcrlf)");
    va = values[d];
    for(var c = 0;c < names.length;c++)
    {
        txtstream.WriteLine("Response.Write(\"<td        style='color:navy;font-
size:10px;font-family:Cambria, serif;' align='left' nowrap>" + va[c] + "</td>\" &
vbcrlf)");
    }
    txtstream.WriteLine("Response.Write(\"</tr>\" & vbcrlf)");
}
```

Horizontal Using A Button

```
for(var d = 0;d < values.length;d++)
{
    txtstream.WriteLine("Response.Write(\"<tr>\" & vbcrlf)");
    va = values[d];
    for(var c = 0;c < names.length;c++)
    {
        txtstream.WriteLine("Response.Write(\"<td        style='color:navy;font-
size:10px;font-family:Cambria, serif;' align='left' nowrap><input Type= button
value=\"\" + va[c] + \"\"\"></input></td>\" & vbcrlf)");
    }
    txtstream.WriteLine("Response.Write(\"</tr>\" & vbcrlf)");
}
```

Horizontal Using A ComboBox

```
for(var d = 0;d < values.length;d++)
{
    txtstream.WriteLine("Response.Write(\"<tr>\" & vbcrlf)");
```

```
        va = values[d];
        for(var c = 0;c < names.length;c++)
        {
            txtstream.WriteLine("Response.Write(\"<td style='font-family:Calibri, Sans-
Serif;font-size: 12px;color:navy;' align='left' nowrap='true'><select><option value =
'" + va[c] + "'>" + va[c] + "</option></select></td>\" + vbcrlf)");
        }
        txtstream.WriteLine("Response.Write(\"</tr>\" & vbcrlf)");
    }
```

Horizontal Using A Div

```
    for(var d = 0;d < values.length;d++)
    {
            txtstream.WriteLine("Response.Write(\"<tr>\" & vbcrlf)");
            va = values[d];
            for(var c = 0;c < names.length;c++)
            {

                txtstream.WriteLine("Response.Write(\"<td        style='color:navy;font-
size:10px;font-family:Cambria,   serif;'  align='left'  nowrap><div>" + va[c] +
"</div></td>\" & vbcrlf)");

            }
            txtstream.WriteLine("Response.Write(\"</tr>\" & vbcrlf)");
    }
```

Horizontal Using A Link

```
    for(var d = 0;d < values.length;d++)
    {
        txtstream.WriteLine("Response.Write(\"<tr>\" & vbcrlf)");
        va = values[d];
        for(var c = 0;c < names.length;c++)
        {
```

```
        txtstream.WriteLine("Response.Write(\"<td style='font-family:Calibri, Sans-
Serif;font-size: 12px;color:navy;' align='left' nowrap='true'><a href='" + va[c] +
"'>" + va[c] + "</a></td>\" + vbcrlf)");
    }
    txtstream.WriteLine("Response.Write(\"</tr>\" & vbcrlf)");
  }
```

Horizontal Using A ListBox

```
  for(var d = 0;d < values.length;d++

  {

    txtstream.WriteLine("Response.Write(\"<tr>\" & vbcrlf)");

    va = values[d];
    for(var c = 0;c < names.length;c++)
    {
        txtstream.WriteLine("Response.Write(\"<td style='font-family:Calibri, Sans-
Serif;font-size:      12px;color:navy;'      align='left'      nowrap='true'><select
multiple><option value = '" + va[c] + "'>" + va[c] + "</option></select></td>\" +
vbcrlf)");
    }
    txtstream.WriteLine("Response.Write(\"</tr>\" & vbcrlf)");
  }
```

Horizontal Using A Span

```
  for(var d = 0;d < values.length;d++

  {

    txtstream.WriteLine("Response.Write(\"<tr>\" & vbcrlf)");

    va = values[d];
    for(var c = 0;c < names.length;c++)
    {
        txtstream.WriteLine("Response.Write(\"<td            style='color:navy;font-
size:10px;font-family:Cambria, serif;' align='left' nowrap><span>" + va[c] +
"</span></td>\" & vbcrlf)");
    }
    txtstream.WriteLine("Response.Write(\"</tr>\" & vbcrlf)");
```

```
    }
```

Horizontal Using A Textarea

```
for(var d = 0;d < values.length;d++

{

    txtstream.WriteLine("Response.Write(\"<tr>\" & vbcrlf)");

    va = values[d];
    for(var c = 0;c < names.length;c++)
    {
        txtstream.WriteLine("Response.Write(\"<td          style='color:navy;font-
size:10px;font-family:Cambria, serif;' align='left' nowrap><textarea>" + va[c] +
"</textarea></td>\" & vbcrlf)");
    }
    txtstream.WriteLine("Response.Write(\"</tr>\" & vbcrlf)");
}
```

Horizontal Using A TextBox

```
for(var d = 0;d < values.length;d++

{

    txtstream.WriteLine("Response.Write(\"<tr>\" & vbcrlf)");

    va = values[d];
    for(var c = 0;c < names.length;c++)
    {
        txtstream.WriteLine("Response.Write(\"<td          style='color:navy;font-
size:10px;font-family:Cambria, serif;' align='left' nowrap><input   Type=text
value=\"\" + va[c] + \"\"></input></td>\" & vbcrlf)");

    }
    txtstream.WriteLine("Response.Write(\"</tr>\" & vbcrlf)");
}
```

Vertical No Additional Controls

```
for(var c = 0;c < names.length;c++)
{
    txtstream.WriteLine("Response.Write(\"<tr><th        style='color:darkred;font-size:10px;font-family:Cambria, serif;' align='left' nowrap>" + names[c] + "</th>\" & vbcrlf)");
    for(var d = 0;d < values.length;d++)
    {
      va = values[d];
        txtstream.WriteLine("Response.Write(\"<td            style='color:navy;font-size:10px;font-family:Cambria, serif;' align='left' nowrap>" + va[c] + "</td>\" & vbcrlf)");
    }
    txtstream.WriteLine("Response.Write(\"</tr>\" & vbcrlf)");
}
```

Vertical Using A Button

```
for(var c = 0;c < names.length;c++)
{
    txtstream.WriteLine("Response.Write(\"<tr><th        style='color:darkred;font-size:10px;font-family:Cambria, serif;' align='left' nowrap>" + names[c] + "</th>\" & vbcrlf)");
    for(var d = 0;d < values.length;d++)
    {
      va = values[d];
        txtstream.WriteLine("Response.Write(\"<td            style='color:navy;font-size:10px;font-family:Cambria, serif;' align='left' nowrap><input Type= button value=\"\" + va[c] + \"\"></input></td>\" & vbcrlf)");
    }
    txtstream.WriteLine("Response.Write(\"</tr>\" & vbcrlf)");
}
```

Vertical Using A ComboBox

```
for(var c = 0;c < names.length;c++)
{
    txtstream.WriteLine("Response.Write(\"<tr><th         style='color:darkred;font-
size:10px;font-family:Cambria, serif;' align='left' nowrap>" + names[c] + "</th>\"
& vbcrlf)");
    for(var d = 0;d < values.length;d++)
    {
        va = values[d];
        txtstream.WriteLine("Response.Write(\"<td style='font-family:Calibri, Sans-
Serif;font-size: 12px;color:navy;' align='left' nowrap='true'><select><option value =
'" + va[c] + "'>" + va[c] + "</option></select></td>\" + vbcrlf)");
    }
    txtstream.WriteLine("Response.Write(\"</tr>\" & vbcrlf)");
}
```

Vertical Using A Div

```
for(var c = 0;c < names.length;c++)
{
    txtstream.WriteLine("Response.Write(\"<tr><th         style='color:darkred;font-
size:10px;font-family:Cambria, serif;' align='left' nowrap>" + names[c] + "</th>\"
& vbcrlf)");
    for(var d = 0;d < values.length;d++)
    {
        va = values[d];
        txtstream.WriteLine("Response.Write(\"<td                   style='color:navy;font-
size:10px;font-family:Cambria,  serif;'  align='left'  nowrap><div>"  +  va[c]  +
"</div></td>\" & vbcrlf)");
    }
    txtstream.WriteLine("Response.Write(\"</tr>\" & vbcrlf)")
}
```

Vertical Using A Link

```
for(var c = 0;c < names.length;c++)
{
```

```
    txtstream.WriteLine("Response.Write(\"<tr><th       style='color:darkred;font-
size:10px;font-family:Cambria, serif;' align='left' nowrap>" + names[c] + "</th>\"
& vbcrlf)");
    for(var d = 0;d < values.length;d++)
    {
      va = values[d];
      txtstream.WriteLine("Response.Write(\"<td style='font-family:Calibri, Sans-
Serif;font-size: 12px;color:navy;' align='left' nowrap='true'><a href='" + va[c] +
"'>" + va[c] + "</a></td>\" + vbcrlf)");
    }
    txtstream.WriteLine("Response.Write(\"</tr>\" & vbcrlf)");
  }
```

Vertical Using A ListBox

```
  for(var c = 0;c < names.length;c++)
  {
    txtstream.WriteLine("Response.Write(\"<tr><th       style='color:darkred;font-
size:10px;font-family:Cambria, serif;' align='left' nowrap>" + names[c] + "</th>\"
& vbcrlf)");
    for(var d = 0;d < values.length;d++)
    {
      va = values[d];
      txtstream.WriteLine("Response.Write(\"<td style='font-family:Calibri, Sans-
Serif;font-size:     12px;color:navy;'     align='left'     nowrap='true'><select
multiple><option value = '" + va[c] + "'>" + va[c] + "</option></select></td>\" +
vbcrlf)");
    }
    txtstream.WriteLine("Response.Write(\"</tr>\" & vbcrlf)");
  }
```

Vertical Using A Span

```
  for(var c = 0;c < names.length;c++)
  {
    txtstream.WriteLine("Response.Write(\"<tr><th       style='color:darkred;font-
size:10px;font-family:Cambria, serif;' align='left' nowrap>" + names[c] + "</th>\"
& vbcrlf)");
    for(var d = 0;d < values.length;d++)
    {
```

```
    va = values[d];
    txtstream.WriteLine("Response.Write(\"<td          style='color:navy;font-
size:10px;font-family:Cambria,  serif;'  align='left'  nowrap><span>" + va[c] +
"</span></td>\" & vbcrlf)");
    }
    txtstream.WriteLine("Response.Write(\"</tr>\" & vbcrlf)");
}
```

Vertical Using A Textarea

```
for(var c = 0;c < names.length;c++)
{
    txtstream.WriteLine("Response.Write(\"<tr><th         style='color:darkred;font-
size:10px;font-family:Cambria, serif;' align='left' nowrap>" + names[c] + "</th>\"
& vbcrlf)");
    for(var d = 0;d < values.length;d++)
    {
        va = values[d];
        txtstream.WriteLine("Response.Write(\"<td          style='color:navy;font-
size:10px;font-family:Cambria,  serif;'  align='left'  nowrap><textarea>" + va[c] +
"</textarea></td>\" & vbcrlf)");
    }
    txtstream.WriteLine("Response.Write(\"</tr>\" & vbcrlf)");
}
```

Vertical Using A TextBox

```
for(var c = 0;c < names.length;c++)
{
    txtstream.WriteLine("Response.Write(\"<tr><th         style='color:darkred;font-
size:10px;font-family:Cambria, serif;' align='left' nowrap>" + names[c] + "</th>\"
& vbcrlf)");
    for(var d = 0;d < values.length;d++)
    {
        va = values[d];
        txtstream.WriteLine("Response.Write(\"<td          style='color:navy;font-
size:10px;font-family:Cambria,   serif;'   align='left'   nowrap><input   Type=text
value=\"\" + va[c] + \"\"></input></td>\" & vbcrlf)");
    }
```

```
    txtstream.WriteLine("Response.Write(\"</tr>\" & vbcrlf)");
}
```

End Code

```
    txtstream.WriteLine("Response.Write(\"</table>\" & vbcrlf)");
    txtstream.WriteLine("%>");
    txtstream.WriteLine("</body>");
    txtstream.WriteLine("</html>");
    txtstream.Close();

}
```

ASPX Reports

Begin Code

```
var ws = new ActiveXObject("WScript.Shell");
var filename = ws.CurrentDirectory + "\\Win32_Process.aspx";
var fso = new ActiveXObject("Scripting.FileSystemObject");
var txtstream = fso.OpenTextFile(filename, 2, true, -2);
txtstream.writeline("<!DOCTYPE html PUBLIC \"-//W3C//DTD XHTML 1.0
Transitional//EN\"                \"http://www.w3.org/TR/xhtml1/DTD/xhtml1-
transitional.dtd\">");
txtstream.writeline("");
txtstream.writeline("<html xmlns=\"http://www.w3.org/1999/xhtml\">");
txtstream.WriteLine("<head>");
txtstream.WriteLine("<title>Win32_Process</title>");
txtstream.WriteLine("</head>");
txtstream.WriteLine("<body>");
txtstream.WriteLine("<%");
txtstream.WriteLine("Response.Write(\"<table                cellpadding=2
cellspacing=2>\" & vbcrlf)");
```

Horizontal Views

```
txtstream.WriteLine("Response.Write(\"<tr>\" & vbcrlf)");
```

```
        for(var c = 0;c < names.length;c++)
        {
                txtstream.WriteLine("Response.Write(\"<th        style='color:darkred;font-size:10px;font-family:Cambria, serif;' align='left' nowrap>" + names[c] + "</th>\" & vbcrlf)");
        }
        txtstream.WriteLine("Response.Write(\"</tr>\" & vbcrlf)");
```

Horizontal No Additional Tags

```
    for(var d = 0;d < values.length;d++)
    {
        txtstream.WriteLine("Response.Write(\"<tr>\" & vbcrlf)");
        va = values[d];
        for(var c = 0;c < names.length;c++)
        {
                txtstream.WriteLine("Response.Write(\"<td        style='color:navy;font-size:10px;font-family:Cambria, serif;' align='left' nowrap>" + va[c] + "</td>\" & vbcrlf)");
        }
        txtstream.WriteLine("Response.Write(\"</tr>\" & vbcrlf)");
    }
```

Horizontal Using A Button

```
    for(var d = 0;d < values.length;d++)
    {
        txtstream.WriteLine("Response.Write(\"<tr>\" & vbcrlf)");
        va = values[d];
        for(var c = 0;c < names.length;c++)
        {
                txtstream.WriteLine("Response.Write(\"<td        style='color:navy;font-size:10px;font-family:Cambria, serif;' align='left' nowrap><input Type= button value=\"\" + va[c] + \"\"\"></input></td>\" & vbcrlf)");
        }
        txtstream.WriteLine("Response.Write(\"</tr>\" & vbcrlf)");
    }
```

Horizontal Using A ComboBox

```
for(var d = 0;d < values.length;d++)
{
    txtstream.WriteLine("Response.Write(\"<tr>\" & vbcrlf)");
    va = values[d];
    for(var c = 0;c < names.length;c++)
    {
        txtstream.WriteLine("Response.Write(\"<td style='font-family:Calibri, Sans-Serif;font-size: 12px;color:navy;' align='left' nowrap='true'><select><option value = '" + va[c] + "'>" + va[c] + "</option></select></td>\" + vbcrlf)");
    }
    txtstream.WriteLine("Response.Write(\"</tr>\" & vbcrlf)");
}
```

Horizontal Using A Div

```
for(var d = 0;d < values.length;d++)
{
        txtstream.WriteLine("Response.Write(\"<tr>\" & vbcrlf)");
        va = values[d];
        for(var c = 0;c < names.length;c++)
        {

            txtstream.WriteLine("Response.Write(\"<td           style='color:navy;font-size:10px;font-family:Cambria,   serif;'   align='left'   nowrap><div>" + va[c] + "</div></td>\" & vbcrlf)");

        }
    txtstream.WriteLine("Response.Write(\"</tr>\" & vbcrlf)");
}
```

Horizontal Using A Link

```
for(var d = 0;d < values.length;d++)
{
    txtstream.WriteLine("Response.Write(\"<tr>\" & vbcrlf)");
    va = values[d];
    for(var c = 0;c < names.length;c++)
    {
        txtstream.WriteLine("Response.Write(\"<td style='font-family:Calibri, Sans-
Serif;font-size: 12px;color:navy;' align='left' nowrap='true'><a href='" + va[c] +
"'>" + va[c] + "</a></td>\" + vbcrlf)");
    }
    txtstream.WriteLine("Response.Write(\"</tr>\" & vbcrlf)");
}
```

Horizontal Using A ListBox

```
for(var d = 0;d < values.length;d++

{

    txtstream.WriteLine("Response.Write(\"<tr>\" & vbcrlf)");

    va = values[d];
    for(var c = 0;c < names.length;c++)
    {
        txtstream.WriteLine("Response.Write(\"<td style='font-family:Calibri, Sans-
Serif;font-size:     12px;color:navy;'     align='left'     nowrap='true'><select
multiple><option value = '" + va[c] + "'>" + va[c] + "</option></select></td>\" +
vbcrlf)");
    }
    txtstream.WriteLine("Response.Write(\"</tr>\" & vbcrlf)");
}
```

Horizontal Using A Span

```
for(var d = 0;d < values.length;d++

{

    txtstream.WriteLine("Response.Write(\"<tr>\" & vbcrlf)");

    va = values[d];
    for(var c = 0;c < names.length;c++)
```

```
    {
        txtstream.WriteLine("Response.Write(\"<td          style='color:navy;font-
size:10px;font-family:Cambria, serif;' align='left' nowrap><span>" + va[c] +
"</span></td>\" & vbcrlf)");
    }
    txtstream.WriteLine("Response.Write(\"</tr>\" & vbcrlf)");
}
```

Horizontal Using A Textarea

```
for(var d = 0;d < values.length;d++

{

    txtstream.WriteLine("Response.Write(\"<tr>\" & vbcrlf)");

    va = values[d];
    for(var c = 0;c < names.length;c++)
    {
        txtstream.WriteLine("Response.Write(\"<td          style='color:navy;font-
size:10px;font-family:Cambria, serif;' align='left' nowrap><textarea>" + va[c] +
"</textarea></td>\" & vbcrlf)");
    }
    txtstream.WriteLine("Response.Write(\"</tr>\" & vbcrlf)");
}
```

Horizontal Using A TextBox

```
for(var d = 0;d < values.length;d++

{

    txtstream.WriteLine("Response.Write(\"<tr>\" & vbcrlf)");

    va = values[d];
    for(var c = 0;c < names.length;c++)
    {
        txtstream.WriteLine("Response.Write(\"<td          style='color:navy;font-
size:10px;font-family:Cambria, serif;' align='left' nowrap><input  Type=text
value=\"\" + va[c] + \"\"></input></td>\" & vbcrlf)");
```

```
    }
    txtstream.WriteLine("Response.Write(\"</tr>\" & vbcrlf)");
}
```

Vertical No Additional Controls

```
for(var c = 0;c < names.length;c++)
{
    txtstream.WriteLine("Response.Write(\"<tr><th        style='color:darkred;font-
size:10px;font-family:Cambria, serif;' align='left' nowrap>" + names[c] + "</th>\"
& vbcrlf)");
    for(var d = 0;d < values.length;d++)
    {
      va = values[d];
        txtstream.WriteLine("Response.Write(\"<td              style='color:navy;font-
size:10px;font-family:Cambria, serif;' align='left' nowrap>" + va[c] + "</td>\" &
vbcrlf)");
    }
    txtstream.WriteLine("Response.Write(\"</tr>\" & vbcrlf)");
}
```

Vertical Using A Button

```
for(var c = 0;c < names.length;c++)
{
    txtstream.WriteLine("Response.Write(\"<tr><th        style='color:darkred;font-
size:10px;font-family:Cambria, serif;' align='left' nowrap>" + names[c] + "</th>\"
& vbcrlf)");
    for(var d = 0;d < values.length;d++)
    {
      va = values[d];
        txtstream.WriteLine("Response.Write(\"<td              style='color:navy;font-
size:10px;font-family:Cambria, serif;' align='left' nowrap><input Type= button
value=\"\" + va[c] + \"\"\"></input></td>\" & vbcrlf)");
    }
    txtstream.WriteLine("Response.Write(\"</tr>\" & vbcrlf)");
```

```
    }
```

Vertical Using A ComboBox

```
for(var c = 0;c < names.length;c++)
{
    txtstream.WriteLine("Response.Write(\"<tr><th       style='color:darkred;font-
size:10px;font-family:Cambria, serif;' align='left' nowrap>" + names[c] + "</th>\"
& vbcrlf)");
    for(var d = 0;d < values.length;d++)
    {
      va = values[d];
      txtstream.WriteLine("Response.Write(\"<td style='font-family:Calibri, Sans-
Serif;font-size: 12px;color:navy;' align='left' nowrap='true'><select><option value =
'" + va[c] + "'>" + va[c] + "</option></select></td>\" + vbcrlf)");
    }
    txtstream.WriteLine("Response.Write(\"</tr>\" & vbcrlf)");
}
```

Vertical Using A Div

```
for(var c = 0;c < names.length;c++)
{
    txtstream.WriteLine("Response.Write(\"<tr><th       style='color:darkred;font-
size:10px;font-family:Cambria, serif;' align='left' nowrap>" + names[c] + "</th>\"
& vbcrlf)");
    for(var d = 0;d < values.length;d++)
    {
      va = values[d];
      txtstream.WriteLine("Response.Write(\"<td             style='color:navy;font-
size:10px;font-family:Cambria,  serif;'  align='left'  nowrap><div>"  +  va[c]  +
"</div></td>\" & vbcrlf)");
    }
    txtstream.WriteLine("Response.Write(\"</tr>\" & vbcrlf)")
}
```

Vertical Using A Link

```
for(var c = 0;c < names.length;c++)
{
    txtstream.WriteLine("Response.Write(\"<tr><th          style='color:darkred;font-
size:10px;font-family:Cambria, serif;' align='left' nowrap>" + names[c] + "</th>\"
& vbcrlf)");
    for(var d = 0;d < values.length;d++)
    {
      va = values[d];
    txtstream.WriteLine("Response.Write(\"<td style='font-family:Calibri, Sans-
Serif;font-size: 12px;color:navy;' align='left' nowrap='true'><a href='" + va[c] +
"'>" + va[c] + "</a></td>\" + vbcrlf)");
    }
    txtstream.WriteLine("Response.Write(\"</tr>\" & vbcrlf)");
}
```

Vertical Using A ListBox

```
for(var c = 0;c < names.length;c++)
{
    txtstream.WriteLine("Response.Write(\"<tr><th          style='color:darkred;font-
size:10px;font-family:Cambria, serif;' align='left' nowrap>" + names[c] + "</th>\"
& vbcrlf)");
    for(var d = 0;d < values.length;d++)
    {
      va = values[d];
    txtstream.WriteLine("Response.Write(\"<td style='font-family:Calibri, Sans-
Serif;font-size:      12px;color:navy;'      align='left'      nowrap='true'><select
multiple><option value = '" + va[c] + "'>" + va[c] + "</option></select></td>\" +
vbcrlf)");
    }
    txtstream.WriteLine("Response.Write(\"</tr>\" & vbcrlf)");
}
```

Vertical Using A Span

```
for(var c = 0;c < names.length;c++)
{
```

```
txtstream.WriteLine("Response.Write(\"<tr><th        style='color:darkred;font-
size:10px;font-family:Cambria, serif;' align='left' nowrap>" + names[c] + "</th>\"
& vbcrlf)");
    for(var d = 0;d < values.length;d++)
    {
        va = values[d];
        txtstream.WriteLine("Response.Write(\"<td           style='color:navy;font-
size:10px;font-family:Cambria, serif;' align='left' nowrap><span>" + va[c] +
"</span></td>\" & vbcrlf)");
    }
    txtstream.WriteLine("Response.Write(\"</tr>\" & vbcrlf)");
}
```

Vertical Using A Textarea

```
for(var c = 0;c < names.length;c++)
{
    txtstream.WriteLine("Response.Write(\"<tr><th        style='color:darkred;font-
size:10px;font-family:Cambria, serif;' align='left' nowrap>" + names[c] + "</th>\"
& vbcrlf)");
    for(var d = 0;d < values.length;d++)
    {
        va = values[d];
        txtstream.WriteLine("Response.Write(\"<td           style='color:navy;font-
size:10px;font-family:Cambria, serif;' align='left' nowrap><textarea>" + va[c] +
"</textarea></td>\" & vbcrlf)");
    }
    txtstream.WriteLine("Response.Write(\"</tr>\" & vbcrlf)");
}
```

Vertical Using A TextBox

```
for(var c = 0;c < names.length;c++)
{
    txtstream.WriteLine("Response.Write(\"<tr><th        style='color:darkred;font-
size:10px;font-family:Cambria, serif;' align='left' nowrap>" + names[c] + "</th>\"
& vbcrlf)");
    for(var d = 0;d < values.length;d++)
    {
```

```
    va = values[d];
    txtstream.WriteLine("Response.Write(\"<td              style='color:navy;font-
size:10px;font-family:Cambria,   serif;'   align='left'   nowrap><input   Type=text
value=\"\" + va[c] + \"\"></input></td>\" & vbcrlf)");
    }
    txtstream.WriteLine("Response.Write(\"</tr>\" & vbcrlf)");
}
```

End Code

```
txtstream.WriteLine("Response.Write(\"</table>\" & vbcrlf)");
txtstream.WriteLine("%>");
txtstream.WriteLine("</body>");
txtstream.WriteLine("</html>");
txtstream.Close();

}
```

ASPX TABLES

```
function Write_The_Code()
{
  var ws = new ActiveXObject("WScript.Shell");
  var filename = ws.CurrentDirectory + "\\Win32_Process.aspx";
  var fso = new ActiveXObject("Scripting.FileSystemObject");
  var txtstream = fso.OpenTextFile(filename, 2, true, -2);
  txtstream.writeline("<html xmlns=\"http://www.w3.org/1999/xhtml\">");
  txtstream.WriteLine("<head>");
  txtstream.WriteLine("<title>Win32_Process</title>");
  txtstream.WriteLine("</head>");
  txtstream.WriteLine("<body>");
  txtstream.WriteLine("<%");
  txtstream.WriteLine("Response.Write(\"<table cellpadding=2 cellspacing=2>\" &
vbcrlf)");
  txtstream.WriteLine("Response.Write(\"<tr>\" & vbcrlf)");
  for(var c = 0;c < names.length;c++)
  {
    txtstream.WriteLine("Response.Write(\"<th          style='color:darkred;font-
size:10px;font-family:Cambria, serif;' align='left' nowrap>" + names[c] + "</th>\"
& vbcrlf)");
```

```
   }
   txtstream.WriteLine("Response.Write(\"</tr>\" & vbcrlf)");
```

Horizontal No Additional Tags

```
for(var d = 0;d < values.length;d++)
{
   txtstream.WriteLine("Response.Write(\"<tr>\" & vbcrlf)");
   va = values[d];
   for(var c = 0;c < names.length;c++)
   {
       txtstream.WriteLine("Response.Write(\"<td          style='color:navy;font-
size:10px;font-family:Cambria, serif;' align='left' nowrap>" + va[c] + "</td>\" &
vbcrlf)");
   }
   txtstream.WriteLine("Response.Write(\"</tr>\" & vbcrlf)");
}
```

Horizontal Using A Button

```
for(var d = 0;d < values.length;d++)
{
   txtstream.WriteLine("Response.Write(\"<tr>\" & vbcrlf)");
   va = values[d];
   for(var c = 0;c < names.length;c++)
   {
       txtstream.WriteLine("Response.Write(\"<td          style='color:navy;font-
size:10px;font-family:Cambria, serif;' align='left' nowrap><input Type= button
value=\"\" + va[c] + \"\"></input></td>\" & vbcrlf)");
   }
   txtstream.WriteLine("Response.Write(\"</tr>\" & vbcrlf)");
}
```

Horizontal Using A ComboBox

```
for(var d = 0;d < values.length;d++)
{
```

```
txtstream.WriteLine("Response.Write(\"<tr>\" & vbcrlf)");
va = values[d];
for(var c = 0;c < names.length;c++)
{
    txtstream.WriteLine("Response.Write(\"<td style='font-family:Calibri, Sans-Serif;font-size: 12px;color:navy;' align='left' nowrap='true'><select><option value = '" + va[c] + "'>" + va[c] + "</option></select></td>\" + vbcrlf)");
}
txtstream.WriteLine("Response.Write(\"</tr>\" & vbcrlf)");
}
```

Horizontal Using A Div

```
for(var d = 0;d < values.length;d++)
{
    txtstream.WriteLine("Response.Write(\"<tr>\" & vbcrlf)");
    va = values[d];
    for(var c = 0;c < names.length;c++)
    {

    txtstream.WriteLine("Response.Write(\"<td        style='color:navy;font-size:10px;font-family:Cambria,   serif;'  align='left'  nowrap><div>" + va[c] + "</div></td>\" & vbcrlf)");

    }
    txtstream.WriteLine("Response.Write(\"</tr>\" & vbcrlf)");
}
```

Horizontal Using A Link

```
for(var d = 0;d < values.length;d++)
{
    txtstream.WriteLine("Response.Write(\"<tr>\" & vbcrlf)");
    va = values[d];
    for(var c = 0;c < names.length;c++)
    {
        txtstream.WriteLine("Response.Write(\"<td style='font-family:Calibri, Sans-Serif;font-size: 12px;color:navy;' align='left' nowrap='true'><a href='" + va[c] + "'>" + va[c] + "</a></td>\" + vbcrlf)");
```

```
        }
        txtstream.WriteLine("Response.Write(\"</tr>\" & vbcrlf)");
    }
```

Horizontal Using A ListBox

```
    for(var d = 0;d < values.length;d++

    {

        txtstream.WriteLine("Response.Write(\"<tr>\" & vbcrlf)");

        va = values[d];
        for(var c = 0;c < names.length;c++)
        {
            txtstream.WriteLine("Response.Write(\"<td style='font-family:Calibri, Sans-
Serif;font-size:    12px;color:navy;'    align='left'    nowrap='true'><select
multiple><option value = '" + va[c] + "'>" + va[c] + "</option></select></td>\" +
vbcrlf)");
        }
        txtstream.WriteLine("Response.Write(\"</tr>\" & vbcrlf)");
    }
```

Horizontal Using A Span

```
    for(var d = 0;d < values.length;d++

    {

        txtstream.WriteLine("Response.Write(\"<tr>\" & vbcrlf)");

        va = values[d];
        for(var c = 0;c < names.length;c++)
        {
            txtstream.WriteLine("Response.Write(\"<td            style='color:navy;font-
size:10px;font-family:Cambria,   serif;'  align='left'  nowrap><span>" + va[c] +
"</span></td>\" & vbcrlf)");
        }
        txtstream.WriteLine("Response.Write(\"</tr>\" & vbcrlf)");
    }
```

Horizontal Using A Textarea

```
for(var d = 0;d < values.length;d++

{

    txtstream.WriteLine("Response.Write(\"<tr>\" & vbcrlf)");

    va = values[d];
    for(var c = 0;c < names.length;c++)
    {
        txtstream.WriteLine("Response.Write(\"<td                 style='color:navy;font-
size:10px;font-family:Cambria,  serif;'  align='left'  nowrap><textarea>" + va[c] +
"</textarea></td>\" & vbcrlf)");
    }
    txtstream.WriteLine("Response.Write(\"</tr>\" & vbcrlf)");
}
```

Horizontal Using A TextBox

```
for(var d = 0;d < values.length;d++

{

    txtstream.WriteLine("Response.Write(\"<tr>\" & vbcrlf)");

    va = values[d];
    for(var c = 0;c < names.length;c++)
    {
        txtstream.WriteLine("Response.Write(\"<td                 style='color:navy;font-
size:10px;font-family:Cambria,   serif;'   align='left'   nowrap><input   Type=text
value=\"\" + va[c] + \"\"></input></td>\" & vbcrlf)");

    }
    txtstream.WriteLine("Response.Write(\"</tr>\" & vbcrlf)");
}
```

Vertical No Additional Controls

```
for(var c = 0;c < names.length;c++)
{
    txtstream.WriteLine("Response.Write(\"<tr><th         style='color:darkred;font-
size:10px;font-family:Cambria, serif;' align='left' nowrap>" + names[c] + "</th>\"
& vbcrlf)");
    for(var d = 0;d < values.length;d++)
    {
        va = values[d];
        txtstream.WriteLine("Response.Write(\"<td             style='color:navy;font-
size:10px;font-family:Cambria, serif;' align='left' nowrap>" + va[c] + "</td>\" &
vbcrlf)");
    }
    txtstream.WriteLine("Response.Write(\"</tr>\" & vbcrlf)");
}
```

Vertical Using A Button

```
for(var c = 0;c < names.length;c++)
{
    txtstream.WriteLine("Response.Write(\"<tr><th         style='color:darkred;font-
size:10px;font-family:Cambria, serif;' align='left' nowrap>" + names[c] + "</th>\"
& vbcrlf)");
    for(var d = 0;d < values.length;d++)
    {
        va = values[d];
        txtstream.WriteLine("Response.Write(\"<td             style='color:navy;font-
size:10px;font-family:Cambria, serif;' align='left' nowrap><input Type= button
value=\"\" + va[c] + \"\"></input></td>\" & vbcrlf)");
    }
    txtstream.WriteLine("Response.Write(\"</tr>\" & vbcrlf)");
}
```

Vertical Using A ComboBox

```
for(var c = 0;c < names.length;c++)
{
    txtstream.WriteLine("Response.Write(\"<tr><th        style='color:darkred;font-
size:10px;font-family:Cambria, serif;' align='left' nowrap>" + names[c] + "</th>\"
& vbcrlf)");
    for(var d = 0;d < values.length;d++)
    {
        va = values[d];
        txtstream.WriteLine("Response.Write(\"<td style='font-family:Calibri, Sans-
Serif;font-size: 12px;color:navy;' align='left' nowrap='true'><select><option value =
'" + va[c] + "'>" + va[c] + "</option></select></td>\" + vbcrlf)");
    }
    txtstream.WriteLine("Response.Write(\"</tr>\" & vbcrlf)");
}
```

Vertical Using A Div

```
for(var c = 0;c < names.length;c++)
{
    txtstream.WriteLine("Response.Write(\"<tr><th        style='color:darkred;font-
size:10px;font-family:Cambria, serif;' align='left' nowrap>" + names[c] + "</th>\"
& vbcrlf)");
    for(var d = 0;d < values.length;d++)
    {
        va = values[d];
        txtstream.WriteLine("Response.Write(\"<td              style='color:navy;font-
size:10px;font-family:Cambria,  serif;'  align='left'  nowrap><div>"  +  va[c]  +
"</div></td>\" & vbcrlf)");
    }
    txtstream.WriteLine("Response.Write(\"</tr>\" & vbcrlf)")
}
```

Vertical Using A Link

```
for(var c = 0;c < names.length;c++)
{
```

```
    txtstream.WriteLine("Response.Write(\"<tr><th       style='color:darkred;font-
size:10px;font-family:Cambria, serif;' align='left' nowrap>" + names[c] + "</th>\"
& vbcrlf)");
      for(var d = 0;d < values.length;d++)
      {
        va = values[d];
        txtstream.WriteLine("Response.Write(\"<td style='font-family:Calibri, Sans-
Serif;font-size: 12px;color:navy;' align='left' nowrap='true'><a href='" + va[c] +
"'>" + va[c] + "</a></td>\" + vbcrlf)");
      }
    txtstream.WriteLine("Response.Write(\"</tr>\" & vbcrlf)");
  }
```

Vertical Using A ListBox

```
  for(var c = 0;c < names.length;c++)
  {
    txtstream.WriteLine("Response.Write(\"<tr><th       style='color:darkred;font-
size:10px;font-family:Cambria, serif;' align='left' nowrap>" + names[c] + "</th>\"
& vbcrlf)");
      for(var d = 0;d < values.length;d++)
      {
        va = values[d];
        txtstream.WriteLine("Response.Write(\"<td style='font-family:Calibri, Sans-
Serif;font-size:      12px;color:navy;'       align='left'        nowrap='true'><select
multiple><option value = '" + va[c] + "'>" + va[c] + "</option></select></td>\" +
vbcrlf)");
      }
    txtstream.WriteLine("Response.Write(\"</tr>\" & vbcrlf)");
  }
```

Vertical Using A Span

```
  for(var c = 0;c < names.length;c++)
  {
    txtstream.WriteLine("Response.Write(\"<tr><th       style='color:darkred;font-
size:10px;font-family:Cambria, serif;' align='left' nowrap>" + names[c] + "</th>\"
& vbcrlf)");
      for(var d = 0;d < values.length;d++)
      {
```

```
    va = values[d];
    txtstream.WriteLine("Response.Write(\"<td          style='color:navy;font-
size:10px;font-family:Cambria, serif;' align='left' nowrap><span>" + va[c] +
"</span></td>\" & vbcrlf)");
    }
    txtstream.WriteLine("Response.Write(\"</tr>\" & vbcrlf)");
  }
```

Vertical Using A Textarea

```
  for(var c = 0;c < names.length;c++)
  {
    txtstream.WriteLine("Response.Write(\"<tr><th          style='color:darkred;font-
size:10px;font-family:Cambria, serif;' align='left' nowrap>" + names[c] + "</th>\"
& vbcrlf)");
    for(var d = 0;d < values.length;d++)
    {
      va = values[d];
      txtstream.WriteLine("Response.Write(\"<td          style='color:navy;font-
size:10px;font-family:Cambria, serif;' align='left' nowrap><textarea>" + va[c] +
"</textarea></td>\" & vbcrlf)");
    }
    txtstream.WriteLine("Response.Write(\"</tr>\" & vbcrlf)");
  }
```

Vertical Using A TextBox

```
  for(var c = 0;c < names.length;c++)
  {
    txtstream.WriteLine("Response.Write(\"<tr><th          style='color:darkred;font-
size:10px;font-family:Cambria, serif;' align='left' nowrap>" + names[c] + "</th>\"
& vbcrlf)");
    for(var d = 0;d < values.length;d++)
    {
      va = values[d];
      txtstream.WriteLine("Response.Write(\"<td          style='color:navy;font-
size:10px;font-family:Cambria,  serif;'  align='left'  nowrap><input  Type=text
value=\"\" + va[c] + \"\"></input></td>\" & vbcrlf)");
    }
```

```
        txtstream.WriteLine("Response.Write(\"</tr>\" & vbcrlf)");
    }
```

End Code

```
    txtstream.WriteLine("Response.Write(\"</table>\" & vbcrlf)");
    txtstream.WriteLine("%>");
    txtstream.WriteLine("</body>");
    txtstream.WriteLine("</html>");
    txtstream.Close();

}
```

Begin Code

```
function Write_The_Code()
{

    var ws = new ActiveXObject("WScript.Shell");
    var filename = ws.CurrentDirectory + "\\Win32_Process.hta";
    var fso = new ActiveXObject("Scripting.FileSystemObject");
    var txtstream = fso.OpenTextFile(filename, 2, true, -2);
    txtstream.writeline("<html>");
    txtstream.WriteLine("<head>");
    txtstream.WriteLine("<HTA:APPLICATION ");
    txtstream.WriteLine(" ID = \"Win32_Process\" ");
    txtstream.WriteLine(" APPLICATIONNAME = \"Win32_Process\" ");
    txtstream.WriteLine(" SCROLL = \"Yes\" ");
    txtstream.WriteLine(" SINGLEINSTANCE = \"yes\" ");
    txtstream.WriteLine(" WINDOWSTATE = \"normal\">");
    txtstream.WriteLine("<title>Win32_Process</title>");
    txtstream.WriteLine("</head>");
    txtstream.WriteLine("<body>");
    txtstream.WriteLine("<table  boder=0 cellpadding=2 cellspacing=2>\" & vbcrlf)");
```

Horizontal No Additional Tags

```
    for(var d = 0;d < values.length;d++)
```

```
    {
      txtstream.WriteLine("<tr>\" & vbcrlf)");
      va = values[d];
      for(var c = 0;c < names.length;c++)
      {
          txtstream.WriteLine("<td                style='color:navy;font-size:10px;font-
family:Cambria, serif;' align='left' nowrap>" + va[c] + "</td>");
      }
      txtstream.WriteLine("</tr>");
    }
```

Horizontal Using A Button

```
  for(var d = 0;d < values.length;d++)
  {
    txtstream.WriteLine("<tr>");
    va = values[d];
    for(var c = 0;c < names.length;c++)
    {
        txtstream.WriteLine("<td                style='color:navy;font-size:10px;font-
family:Cambria, serif;' align='left' nowrap><input Type= button value=\"\" + va[c] +
\"\"></input></td>");
    }
    txtstream.WriteLine("</tr>");
  }
```

Horizontal Using A ComboBox

```
  for(var d = 0;d < values.length;d++)

  {

    txtstream.WriteLine("<tr>");
    va = values[d];
    for(var c = 0;c < names.length;c++)
    {
```

```
        txtstream.WriteLine("<td    style='font-family:Calibri,  Sans-Serif;font-size:
12px;color:navy;' align='left' nowrap='true'><select><option value = '" + va[c] +
"'>" + va[c] + "</option></select></td>\" + vbcrlf)");
    }
    txtstream.WriteLine("</tr>");
  }
```

Horizontal Using A Div

```
  for(var d = 0;d < values.length;d++)
  {
        txtstream.WriteLine("<tr>");
        va = values[d];
        for(var c = 0;c < names.length;c++)
        {

            txtstream.WriteLine("<td            style='color:navy;font-size:10px;font-
family:Cambria, serif;' align='left' nowrap><div>" + va[c] + "</div></td>");

    }
    txtstream.WriteLine("</tr>");
  }
```

Horizontal Using A Link

```
  for(var d = 0;d < values.length;d++)
  {
    txtstream.WriteLine("<tr>");
    va = values[d];
    for(var c = 0;c < names.length;c++)
    {
        txtstream.WriteLine("<td    style='font-family:Calibri,  Sans-Serif;font-size:
12px;color:navy;' align='left' nowrap='true'><a href='" + va[c] + "'>" + va[c] +
"</a></td>\" + vbcrlf)");
    }
    txtstream.WriteLine("</tr>");
  }
```

Horizontal Using A ListBox

```
for(var d = 0;d < values.length;d++

{

    txtstream.WriteLine("<tr>");

    va = values[d];
    for(var c = 0;c < names.length;c++)
    {
        txtstream.WriteLine("<td    style='font-family:Calibri,    Sans-Serif;font-size:
12px;color:navy;' align='left' nowrap='true'><select multiple><option value = '" +
va[c] + "'>" + va[c] + "</option></select></td>\" + vbcrlf)");
    }
    txtstream.WriteLine("</tr>");
}
```

Horizontal Using A Span

```
for(var d = 0;d < values.length;d++

{

    txtstream.WriteLine("<tr>");

    va = values[d];
    for(var c = 0;c < names.length;c++)
    {
        txtstream.WriteLine("<td                style='color:navy;font-size:10px;font-
family:Cambria, serif;' align='left' nowrap><span>" + va[c] + "</span></td>");
    }
    txtstream.WriteLine("</tr>");
}
```

Horizontal Using A Textarea

```
for(var d = 0;d < values.length;d++

{
```

```
txtstream.WriteLine("<tr>");

va = values[d];
for(var c = 0;c < names.length;c++)
{
    txtstream.WriteLine("<td          style='color:navy;font-size:10px;font-
family:Cambria,    serif;'    align='left'    nowrap><textarea>"    +    va[c]    +
"</textarea></td>");
}
txtstream.WriteLine("</tr>");
}
```

Horizontal Using A TextBox

```
for(var d = 0;d < values.length;d++

{

txtstream.WriteLine("<tr>");

va = values[d];
for(var c = 0;c < names.length;c++)
{
    txtstream.WriteLine("<td          style='color:navy;font-size:10px;font-
family:Cambria, serif;' align='left' nowrap><input Type=text value=\"\" + va[c] +
\"\"></input></td>");

}
txtstream.WriteLine("</tr>");
}
```

Vertical No Additional Controls

```
for(var c = 0;c < names.length;c++)
{
    txtstream.WriteLine("<tr><th          style='color:darkred;font-size:10px;font-
family:Cambria, serif;' align='left' nowrap>" + names[c] + "</th>");
    for(var d = 0;d < values.length;d++)
    {
```

```
    va = values[d];
        txtstream.WriteLine("<td                    style='color:navy;font-size:10px;font-
family:Cambria, serif;' align='left' nowrap>" + va[c] + "</td>");
    }
    txtstream.WriteLine("</tr>");
  }
```

Vertical Using A Button

```
  for(var c = 0;c < names.length;c++)
  {
      txtstream.WriteLine("<tr><th                    style='color:darkred;font-size:10px;font-
family:Cambria, serif;' align='left' nowrap>" + names[c] + "</th>");
      for(var d = 0;d < values.length;d++)
      {
        va = values[d];
        txtstream.WriteLine("<td                    style='color:navy;font-size:10px;font-
family:Cambria, serif;' align='left' nowrap><input Type= button value=\"\" + va[c] +
\"\"></input></td>");
      }
      txtstream.WriteLine("</tr>");
  }
```

Vertical Using A ComboBox

```
  for(var c = 0;c < names.length;c++)
  {
      txtstream.WriteLine("<tr><th                style='color:darkred;font-size:10px;font-
family:Cambria, serif;' align='left' nowrap>" + names[c] + "</th>");
      for(var d = 0;d < values.length;d++)
      {
        va = values[d];
        txtstream.WriteLine("<td    style='font-family:Calibri,    Sans-Serif;font-size:
12px;color:navy;' align='left' nowrap='true'><select><option value = '" + va[c] +
"'>" + va[c] + "</option></select></td>\" + vbcrlf)");
      }
      txtstream.WriteLine("</tr>");
  }
```

Vertical Using A Div

```
for(var c = 0;c < names.length;c++)
{
    txtstream.WriteLine("<tr><th          style='color:darkred;font-size:10px;font-
family:Cambria, serif;' align='left' nowrap>" + names[c] + "</th>");
    for(var d = 0;d < values.length;d++)
    {
      va = values[d];
        txtstream.WriteLine("<td                style='color:navy;font-size:10px;font-
family:Cambria, serif;' align='left' nowrap><div>" + va[c] + "</div></td>");
    }
    txtstream.WriteLine("</tr>")
}
```

Vertical Using A Link

```
for(var c = 0;c < names.length;c++)
{
    txtstream.WriteLine("<tr><th          style='color:darkred;font-size:10px;font-
family:Cambria, serif;' align='left' nowrap>" + names[c] + "</th>");
    for(var d = 0;d < values.length;d++)
    {
      va = values[d];
        txtstream.WriteLine("<td   style='font-family:Calibri,   Sans-Serif;font-size:
12px;color:navy;' align='left' nowrap='true'><a href='" + va[c] + "'>" + va[c] +
"</a></td>\" + vbcrlf)");
    }
    txtstream.WriteLine("</tr>");
}
```

Vertical Using A ListBox

```
for(var c = 0;c < names.length;c++)
{
    txtstream.WriteLine("<tr><th          style='color:darkred;font-size:10px;font-
family:Cambria, serif;' align='left' nowrap>" + names[c] + "</th>");
```

```
        for(var d = 0;d < values.length;d++)
        {
          va = values[d];
          txtstream.WriteLine("<td   style='font-family:Calibri,   Sans-Serif;font-size:
12px;color:navy;' align='left' nowrap='true'><select multiple><option value = '" +
va[c] + "'>" + va[c] + "</option></select></td>\" + vbcrlf)");
        }
        txtstream.WriteLine("</tr>");
    }
```

Vertical Using A Span

```
    for(var c = 0;c < names.length;c++)
    {
        txtstream.WriteLine("<tr><th            style='color:darkred;font-size:10px;font-
family:Cambria, serif;' align='left' nowrap>" + names[c] + "</th>");
        for(var d = 0;d < values.length;d++)
        {
          va = values[d];
          txtstream.WriteLine("<td                 style='color:navy;font-size:10px;font-
family:Cambria, serif;' align='left' nowrap><span>" + va[c] + "</span></td>");
        }
        txtstream.WriteLine("</tr>");
    }
```

Vertical Using A Textarea

```
    for(var c = 0;c < names.length;c++)
    {
        txtstream.WriteLine("<tr><th            style='color:darkred;font-size:10px;font-
family:Cambria, serif;' align='left' nowrap>" + names[c] + "</th>");
        for(var d = 0;d < values.length;d++)
        {
          va = values[d];
          txtstream.WriteLine("<td                 style='color:navy;font-size:10px;font-
family:Cambria,    serif;'    align='left'    nowrap><textarea>"    +    va[c]    +
"</textarea></td>");
        }
        txtstream.WriteLine("</tr>");
    }
```

Vertical Using A TextBox

```
for(var c = 0;c < names.length;c++)
{
    txtstream.WriteLine("<tr><th          style='color:darkred;font-size:10px;font-
family:Cambria, serif;' align='left' nowrap>" + names[c] + "</th>");
    for(var d = 0;d < values.length;d++)
    {
        va = values[d];
        txtstream.WriteLine("<td          style='color:navy;font-size:10px;font-
family:Cambria, serif;' align='left' nowrap><input Type=text value=\"\" + va[c] +
\"\"></input></td>");
    }
    txtstream.WriteLine("</tr>");
}
```

End Code

```
txtstream.WriteLine("</table>");
txtstream.WriteLine("</body>");
txtstream.WriteLine("</html>");
txtstream.Close();
}
```

HTA TABLES

Begin Code

```
function Write_The_Code()
{

    var ws = new ActiveXObject("WScript.Shell");
    var filename = ws.CurrentDirectory + "\\Win32_Process.hta";
    var fso = new ActiveXObject("Scripting.FileSystemObject");
    var txtstream = fso.OpenTextFile(filename, 2, true, -2);
    txtstream.writeline("<html>");
    txtstream.WriteLine("<head>");
    txtstream.WriteLine("<HTA:APPLICATION ");
    txtstream.WriteLine(" ID = \"Win32_Process\" ");
    txtstream.WriteLine(" APPLICATIONNAME = \"Win32_Process\" ");
    txtstream.WriteLine(" SCROLL = \"Yes\" ");
    txtstream.WriteLine(" SINGLEINSTANCE = \"yes\" ");
    txtstream.WriteLine(" WINDOWSTATE = \"normal\">");
    txtstream.WriteLine("<title>Win32_Process</title>");
    txtstream.WriteLine("</head>");
    txtstream.WriteLine("<body>");
    txtstream.WriteLine("<table  boder=1 cellpadding=2 cellspacing=2>");
```

Horizontal No Additional Tags

```
for(var d = 0;d < values.length;d++)
{
    txtstream.WriteLine("<tr>");
    va = values[d];
    for(var c = 0;c < names.length;c++)
    {
        txtstream.WriteLine("<td            style='color:navy;font-size:10px;font-
family:Cambria, serif;' align='left' nowrap>" + va[c] + "</td>");
    }
    txtstream.WriteLine("</tr>");
}
```

Horizontal Using A Button

```
for(var d = 0;d < values.length;d++)
{
    txtstream.WriteLine("<tr>");
    va = values[d];
    for(var c = 0;c < names.length;c++)
    {
        txtstream.WriteLine("<td            style='color:navy;font-size:10px;font-
family:Cambria, serif;' align='left' nowrap><input Type= button value=\"\" + va[c] +
\"\"></input></td>");
    }
    txtstream.WriteLine("</tr>");
}
```

Horizontal Using A ComboBox

```
for(var d = 0;d < values.length;d++)

{

    txtstream.WriteLine("<tr>");
    va = values[d];
```

```
for(var c = 0;c < names.length;c++)
{
     txtstream.WriteLine("<td   style='font-family:Calibri,   Sans-Serif;font-size:
12px;color:navy;' align='left' nowrap='true'><select><option value = '" + va[c] +
"'>" + va[c] + "</option></select></td>\" + vbcrlf)");
}
txtstream.WriteLine("</tr>");
}
```

Horizontal Using A Div

```
for(var d = 0;d < values.length;d++)
{
     txtstream.WriteLine("<tr>");
     va = values[d];
     for(var c = 0;c < names.length;c++)
     {

          txtstream.WriteLine("<td              style='color:navy;font-size:10px;font-
family:Cambria, serif;' align='left' nowrap><div>" + va[c] + "</div></td>");

}
txtstream.WriteLine("</tr>");
}
```

Horizontal Using A Link

```
for(var d = 0;d < values.length;d++)
{
txtstream.WriteLine("<tr>");
va = values[d];
for(var c = 0;c < names.length;c++)
{
     txtstream.WriteLine("<td   style='font-family:Calibri,   Sans-Serif;font-size:
12px;color:navy;' align='left' nowrap='true'><a href='" + va[c] + "'>" + va[c] +
"</a></td>\" + vbcrlf)");
}
```

```
        txtstream.WriteLine("</tr>");
    }
```

Horizontal Using A ListBox

```
    for(var d = 0;d < values.length;d++
    {
        txtstream.WriteLine("<tr>");

        va = values[d];
        for(var c = 0;c < names.length;c++)
        {
            txtstream.WriteLine("<td   style='font-family:Calibri,   Sans-Serif;font-size:
12px;color:navy;' align='left' nowrap='true'><select multiple><option value = '" +
va[c] + "'>" + va[c] + "</option></select></td>\" + vbcrlf)");
        }
        txtstream.WriteLine("</tr>");
    }
```

Horizontal Using A Span

```
    for(var d = 0;d < values.length;d++
    {
        txtstream.WriteLine("<tr>");

        va = values[d];
        for(var c = 0;c < names.length;c++)
        {
            txtstream.WriteLine("<td                style='color:navy;font-size:10px;font-
family:Cambria, serif;' align='left' nowrap><span>" + va[c] + "</span></td>");
        }
        txtstream.WriteLine("</tr>");
    }
```

Horizontal Using A Textarea

```
for(var d = 0;d < values.length;d++

{

  txtstream.WriteLine("<tr>");

  va = values[d];
  for(var c = 0;c < names.length;c++)
  {
      txtstream.WriteLine("<td                style='color:navy;font-size:10px;font-
family:Cambria,    serif;'    align='left'    nowrap><textarea>"    +    va[c]    +
"</textarea></td>");
  }
  txtstream.WriteLine("</tr>");
}
```

Horizontal Using A TextBox

```
for(var d = 0;d < values.length;d++

{

  txtstream.WriteLine("<tr>");

  va = values[d];
  for(var c = 0;c < names.length;c++)
  {
      txtstream.WriteLine("<td                style='color:navy;font-size:10px;font-
family:Cambria, serif;' align='left' nowrap><input Type=text value=\"\" + va[c] +
\"\"></input></td>");

  }
  txtstream.WriteLine("</tr>");
}
```

Vertical No Additional Controls

```
for(var c = 0;c < names.length;c++)
```

```
{
    txtstream.WriteLine("<tr><th          style='color:darkred;font-size:10px;font-
family:Cambria, serif;' align='left' nowrap>" + names[c] + "</th>");
    for(var d = 0;d < values.length;d++)
    {
        va = values[d];
        txtstream.WriteLine("<td              style='color:navy;font-size:10px;font-
family:Cambria, serif;' align='left' nowrap>" + va[c] + "</td>");
    }
    txtstream.WriteLine("</tr>");
}
```

Vertical Using A Button

```
for(var c = 0;c < names.length;c++)
{
    txtstream.WriteLine("<tr><th          style='color:darkred;font-size:10px;font-
family:Cambria, serif;' align='left' nowrap>" + names[c] + "</th>");
    for(var d = 0;d < values.length;d++)
    {
        va = values[d];
        txtstream.WriteLine("<td              style='color:navy;font-size:10px;font-
family:Cambria, serif;' align='left' nowrap><input Type= button value=\"\" + va[c] +
\"\"></input></td>");
    }
    txtstream.WriteLine("</tr>");
}
```

Vertical Using A ComboBox

```
for(var c = 0;c < names.length;c++)
{
    txtstream.WriteLine("<tr><th          style='color:darkred;font-size:10px;font-
family:Cambria, serif;' align='left' nowrap>" + names[c] + "</th>");
    for(var d = 0;d < values.length;d++)
    {
        va = values[d];
```

```
    txtstream.WriteLine("<td    style='font-family:Calibri,   Sans-Serif;font-size:
12px;color:navy;' align='left' nowrap='true'><select><option value = '" + va[c] +
"'>" + va[c] + "</option></select></td>\" + vbcrlf)");
    }
    txtstream.WriteLine("</tr>");
  }
```

Vertical Using A Div

```
  for(var c = 0;c < names.length;c++)
  {
    txtstream.WriteLine("<tr><th           style='color:darkred;font-size:10px;font-
family:Cambria, serif;' align='left' nowrap>" + names[c] + "</th>");
    for(var d = 0;d < values.length;d++)
    {
      va = values[d];
      txtstream.WriteLine("<td              style='color:navy;font-size:10px;font-
family:Cambria, serif;' align='left' nowrap><div>" + va[c] + "</div></td>");
    }
    txtstream.WriteLine("</tr>")
  }
```

Vertical Using A Link

```
  for(var c = 0;c < names.length;c++)
  {
    txtstream.WriteLine("<tr><th           style='color:darkred;font-size:10px;font-
family:Cambria, serif;' align='left' nowrap>" + names[c] + "</th>");
    for(var d = 0;d < values.length;d++)
    {
      va = values[d];
      txtstream.WriteLine("<td    style='font-family:Calibri,   Sans-Serif;font-size:
12px;color:navy;' align='left' nowrap='true'><a href='" + va[c] + "'>" + va[c] +
"</a></td>\" + vbcrlf)");
    }
    txtstream.WriteLine("</tr>");
  }
```

Vertical Using A ListBox

```
for(var c = 0;c < names.length;c++)
{
    txtstream.WriteLine("<tr><th          style='color:darkred;font-size:10px;font-
family:Cambria, serif;' align='left' nowrap>" + names[c] + "</th>");
    for(var d = 0;d < values.length;d++)
    {
      va = values[d];
      txtstream.WriteLine("<td   style='font-family:Calibri,   Sans-Serif;font-size:
12px;color:navy;' align='left' nowrap='true'><select multiple><option value = '" +
va[c] + "'>" + va[c] + "</option></select></td>\" + vbcrlf)");
    }
    txtstream.WriteLine("</tr>");
}
```

Vertical Using A Span

```
for(var c = 0;c < names.length;c++)
{
    txtstream.WriteLine("<tr><th          style='color:darkred;font-size:10px;font-
family:Cambria, serif;' align='left' nowrap>" + names[c] + "</th>");
    for(var d = 0;d < values.length;d++)
    {
      va = values[d];
      txtstream.WriteLine("<td              style='color:navy;font-size:10px;font-
family:Cambria, serif;' align='left' nowrap><span>" + va[c] + "</span></td>");
    }
    txtstream.WriteLine("</tr>");
}
```

Vertical Using A Textarea

```
for(var c = 0;c < names.length;c++)
{
    txtstream.WriteLine("<tr><th          style='color:darkred;font-size:10px;font-
family:Cambria, serif;' align='left' nowrap>" + names[c] + "</th>");
    for(var d = 0;d < values.length;d++)
    {
      va = values[d];
```

```
        txtstream.WriteLine("<td                style='color:navy;font-size:10px;font-
family:Cambria,      serif;'    align='left'    nowrap><textarea>"    +    va[c]    +
"</textarea></td>");
    }
    txtstream.WriteLine("</tr>");
  }
```

Vertical Using A TextBox

```
  for(var c = 0;c < names.length;c++)
  {
        txtstream.WriteLine("<tr><th             style='color:darkred;font-size:10px;font-
family:Cambria, serif;' align='left' nowrap>" + names[c] + "</th>");
      for(var d = 0;d < values.length;d++)
      {
        va = values[d];
        txtstream.WriteLine("<td                style='color:navy;font-size:10px;font-
family:Cambria, serif;' align='left' nowrap><input Type=text value=\"\" + va[c] +
\"\"></input></td>");
    }
    txtstream.WriteLine("</tr>");
  }
```

End Code

```
  txtstream.WriteLine("</table>");
  txtstream.WriteLine("</body>");
  txtstream.WriteLine("</html>");
  txtstream.Close();
}
```

HTML REPORTS

Begin Code

```
function Write_The_Code()
{

    var ws = new ActiveXObject("WScript.Shell");
    var filename = ws.CurrentDirectory + "\\Win32_Process.hta";
    var fso = new ActiveXObject("Scripting.FileSystemObject");
    var txtstream = fso.OpenTextFile(filename, 2, true, -2);
    txtstream.writeline("<html>");
    txtstream.WriteLine("<head>");
    txtstream.WriteLine("<title>Win32_Process</title>");
    txtstream.WriteLine("</head>");
    txtstream.WriteLine("<body>");
    txtstream.WriteLine("<table  boder=0 cellpadding=2 cellspacing=2>");
```

Horizontal No Additional Tags

```
    for(var d = 0;d < values.length;d++)
    {
        txtstream.WriteLine("<tr>");
        va = values[d];
```

```
for(var c = 0;c < names.length;c++)
{
    txtstream.WriteLine("<td                      style='color:navy;font-size:10px;font-
family:Cambria, serif;' align='left' nowrap>" + va[c] + "</td>");
}
txtstream.WriteLine("</tr>");
}
```

Horizontal Using A Button

```
for(var d = 0;d < values.length;d++)
{
    txtstream.WriteLine("<tr>");
    va = values[d];
    for(var c = 0;c < names.length;c++)
    {
        txtstream.WriteLine("<td                      style='color:navy;font-size:10px;font-
family:Cambria, serif;' align='left' nowrap><input Type= button value=\"\" + va[c] +
\"\"></input></td>");
    }
    txtstream.WriteLine("</tr>");
}
```

Horizontal Using A ComboBox

```
for(var d = 0;d < values.length;d++)

{
    txtstream.WriteLine("<tr>");
    va = values[d];
    for(var c = 0;c < names.length;c++)
    {
        txtstream.WriteLine("<td    style='font-family:Calibri,   Sans-Serif;font-size:
12px;color:navy;' align='left' nowrap='true'><select><option value = '" + va[c] +
"'>" + va[c] + "</option></select></td>\" + vbcrlf)");
    }
    txtstream.WriteLine("</tr>");
```

```
        }
```

Horizontal Using A Div

```
    for(var d = 0;d < values.length;d++)
    {
            txtstream.WriteLine("<tr>");
            va = values[d];
            for(var c = 0;c < names.length;c++)
            {

                txtstream.WriteLine("<td          style='color:navy;font-size:10px;font-
family:Cambria, serif;' align='left' nowrap><div>" + va[c] + "</div></td>");

        }
        txtstream.WriteLine("</tr>");
    }
```

Horizontal Using A Link

```
    for(var d = 0;d < values.length;d++)
    {
        txtstream.WriteLine("<tr>");
        va = values[d];
        for(var c = 0;c < names.length;c++)
        {
            txtstream.WriteLine("<td   style='font-family:Calibri,   Sans-Serif;font-size:
12px;color:navy;' align='left' nowrap='true'><a href='" + va[c] + "'>" + va[c] +
"</a></td>\" + vbcrlf)");
        }
        txtstream.WriteLine("</tr>");
    }
```

Horizontal Using A ListBox

```
    for(var d = 0;d < values.length;d++

    {
```

```
    txtstream.WriteLine("<tr>");

    va = values[d];
    for(var c = 0;c < names.length;c++)
    {
        txtstream.WriteLine("<td   style='font-family:Calibri,   Sans-Serif;font-size:
12px;color:navy;' align='left' nowrap='true'><select multiple><option value = '" +
va[c] + "'>" + va[c] + "</option></select></td>\" + vbcrlf)");
    }
    txtstream.WriteLine("</tr>");
}
```

Horizontal Using A Span

```
for(var d = 0;d < values.length;d++

{

    txtstream.WriteLine("<tr>");

    va = values[d];
    for(var c = 0;c < names.length;c++)
    {
        txtstream.WriteLine("<td                    style='color:navy;font-size:10px;font-
family:Cambria, serif;' align='left' nowrap><span>" + va[c] + "</span></td>");
    }
    txtstream.WriteLine("</tr>");
}
```

Horizontal Using A Textarea

```
for(var d = 0;d < values.length;d++

{

    txtstream.WriteLine("<tr>");

    va = values[d];
    for(var c = 0;c < names.length;c++)
```

```
    {
        txtstream.WriteLine("<td            style='color:navy;font-size:10px;font-
family:Cambria,    serif;'    align='left'    nowrap><textarea>"    +    va[c]    +
"</textarea></td>");
    }
    txtstream.WriteLine("</tr>");
 }
```

Horizontal Using A TextBox

```
 for(var d = 0;d < values.length;d++

 {

    txtstream.WriteLine("<tr>");

    va = values[d];
    for(var c = 0;c < names.length;c++)
    {
        txtstream.WriteLine("<td                style='color:navy;font-size:10px;font-
family:Cambria, serif;' align='left' nowrap><input Type=text value=\"\" + va[c] +
\"\"></input></td>");

    }
    txtstream.WriteLine("</tr>");
 }
```

Vertical No Additional Controls

```
 for(var c = 0;c < names.length;c++)
 {
    txtstream.WriteLine("<tr><th          style='color:darkred;font-size:10px;font-
family:Cambria, serif;' align='left' nowrap>" + names[c] + "</th>");
    for(var d = 0;d < values.length;d++)
    {
        va = values[d];
        txtstream.WriteLine("<td              style='color:navy;font-size:10px;font-
family:Cambria, serif;' align='left' nowrap>" + va[c] + "</td>");
```

```
      }
      txtstream.WriteLine("</tr>");
  }
```

Vertical Using A Button

```
  for(var c = 0;c < names.length;c++)
  {
      txtstream.WriteLine("<tr><th          style='color:darkred;font-size:10px;font-
family:Cambria, serif;' align='left' nowrap>" + names[c] + "</th>");
      for(var d = 0;d < values.length;d++)
      {
        va = values[d];
        txtstream.WriteLine("<td              style='color:navy;font-size:10px;font-
family:Cambria, serif;' align='left' nowrap><input Type= button value=\"\" + va[c] +
\"\"></input></td>");
      }
      txtstream.WriteLine("</tr>");
  }
```

Vertical Using A ComboBox

```
  for(var c = 0;c < names.length;c++)
  {
      txtstream.WriteLine("<tr><th          style='color:darkred;font-size:10px;font-
family:Cambria, serif;' align='left' nowrap>" + names[c] + "</th>");
      for(var d = 0;d < values.length;d++)
      {
        va = values[d];
        txtstream.WriteLine("<td    style='font-family:Calibri,   Sans-Serif;font-size:
12px;color:navy;' align='left' nowrap='true'><select><option value = '" + va[c] +
"'>" + va[c] + "</option></select></td>\" + vbcrlf)");
      }
      txtstream.WriteLine("</tr>");
  }
```

Vertical Using A Div

```
for(var c = 0;c < names.length;c++)
{
    txtstream.WriteLine("<tr><th          style='color:darkred;font-size:10px;font-
family:Cambria, serif;' align='left' nowrap>" + names[c] + "</th>");
    for(var d = 0;d < values.length;d++)
    {
      va = values[d];
        txtstream.WriteLine("<td          style='color:navy;font-size:10px;font-
family:Cambria, serif;' align='left' nowrap><div>" + va[c] + "</div></td>");
    }
    txtstream.WriteLine("</tr>")
}
```

Vertical Using A Link

```
for(var c = 0;c < names.length;c++)
{
    txtstream.WriteLine("<tr><th          style='color:darkred;font-size:10px;font-
family:Cambria, serif;' align='left' nowrap>" + names[c] + "</th>");
    for(var d = 0;d < values.length;d++)
    {
      va = values[d];
        txtstream.WriteLine("<td   style='font-family:Calibri,   Sans-Serif;font-size:
12px;color:navy;' align='left' nowrap='true'><a href='" + va[c] + "'>" + va[c] +
"</a></td>\" + vbcrlf)");
    }
    txtstream.WriteLine("</tr>");
}
```

Vertical Using A ListBox

```
for(var c = 0;c < names.length;c++)
{
    txtstream.WriteLine("<tr><th          style='color:darkred;font-size:10px;font-
family:Cambria, serif;' align='left' nowrap>" + names[c] + "</th>");
    for(var d = 0;d < values.length;d++)
```

```
    {
      va = values[d];
      txtstream.WriteLine("<td   style='font-family:Calibri,   Sans-Serif;font-size:
12px;color:navy;' align='left' nowrap='true'><select multiple><option value = '" +
va[c] + "'>" + va[c] + "</option></select></td>\" + vbcrlf)");
    }
    txtstream.WriteLine("</tr>");
  }
```

Vertical Using A Span

```
  for(var c = 0;c < names.length;c++)
  {
      txtstream.WriteLine("<tr><th            style='color:darkred;font-size:10px;font-
family:Cambria, serif;' align='left' nowrap>" + names[c] + "</th>");
      for(var d = 0;d < values.length;d++)
      {
        va = values[d];
        txtstream.WriteLine("<td            style='color:navy;font-size:10px;font-
family:Cambria, serif;' align='left' nowrap><span>" + va[c] + "</span></td>");
      }
      txtstream.WriteLine("</tr>");
  }
```

Vertical Using A Textarea

```
  for(var c = 0;c < names.length;c++)
  {
      txtstream.WriteLine("<tr><th            style='color:darkred;font-size:10px;font-
family:Cambria, serif;' align='left' nowrap>" + names[c] + "</th>");
      for(var d = 0;d < values.length;d++)
      {
        va = values[d];
        txtstream.WriteLine("<td            style='color:navy;font-size:10px;font-
family:Cambria,   serif;'   align='left'   nowrap><textarea>"   +   va[c]   +
"</textarea></td>");
      }
      txtstream.WriteLine("</tr>");
  }
```

Vertical Using A TextBox

```
for(var c = 0;c < names.length;c++)
{
    txtstream.WriteLine("<tr><th          style='color:darkred;font-size:10px;font-
family:Cambria, serif;' align='left' nowrap>" + names[c] + "</th>");
    for(var d = 0;d < values.length;d++)
    {
      va = values[d];
      txtstream.WriteLine("<td              style='color:navy;font-size:10px;font-
family:Cambria, serif;' align='left' nowrap><input Type=text value=\"\" + va[c] +
\"\"></input></td>");
    }
    txtstream.WriteLine("</tr>");
}
```

End Code

```
txtstream.WriteLine("</table>");
txtstream.WriteLine("</body>");
txtstream.WriteLine("</html>");
txtstream.Close();
}
```

HTML TABLES

Begin Code

```
function Write_The_Code()
{

    var ws = new ActiveXObject("WScript.Shell");
    var filename = ws.CurrentDirectory + "\\Win32_Process.hta";
    var fso = new ActiveXObject("Scripting.FileSystemObject");
    var txtstream = fso.OpenTextFile(filename, 2, true, -2);
    txtstream.writeline("<html>");
    txtstream.WriteLine("<head>");
    txtstream.WriteLine("<title>Win32_Process</title>");
    txtstream.WriteLine("</head>");
    txtstream.WriteLine("<body>");
    txtstream.WriteLine("<table  boder=1 cellpadding=2 cellspacing=2>");
```

Horizontal No Additional Tags

```
    for(var d = 0;d < values.length;d++)
    {
        txtstream.WriteLine("<tr>");
        va = values[d];
        for(var c = 0;c < names.length;c++)
        {
```

```
        txtstream.WriteLine("<td                    style='color:navy;font-size:10px;font-
family:Cambria, serif;' align='left' nowrap>" + va[c] + "</td>");
    }
    txtstream.WriteLine("</tr>");
  }
```

Horizontal Using A Button

```
  for(var d = 0;d < values.length;d++)
  {
    txtstream.WriteLine("<tr>");
    va = values[d];
    for(var c = 0;c < names.length;c++)
    {
        txtstream.WriteLine("<td                    style='color:navy;font-size:10px;font-
family:Cambria, serif;' align='left' nowrap><input Type= button value=\"\" + va[c] +
\"\"></input></td>");
    }
    txtstream.WriteLine("</tr>");
  }
```

Horizontal Using A ComboBox

```
  for(var d = 0;d < values.length;d++)

  {

    txtstream.WriteLine("<tr>");
    va = values[d];
    for(var c = 0;c < names.length;c++)
    {
        txtstream.WriteLine("<td    style='font-family:Calibri,    Sans-Serif;font-size:
12px;color:navy;' align='left'  nowrap='true'><select><option value = '" + va[c] +
"'>" + va[c] + "</option></select></td>\" + vbcrlf)");
    }
    txtstream.WriteLine("</tr>");
  }
```

Horizontal Using A Div

```
for(var d = 0;d < values.length;d++)
{
        txtstream.WriteLine("<tr>");
        va = values[d];
        for(var c = 0;c < names.length;c++)
        {

            txtstream.WriteLine("<td        style='color:navy;font-size:10px;font-
family:Cambria, serif;' align='left' nowrap><div>" + va[c] + "</div></td>");

    }
    txtstream.WriteLine("</tr>");
}
```

Horizontal Using A Link

```
for(var d = 0;d < values.length;d++)
{
    txtstream.WriteLine("<tr>");
    va = values[d];
    for(var c = 0;c < names.length;c++)
    {
        txtstream.WriteLine("<td   style='font-family:Calibri,   Sans-Serif;font-size:
12px;color:navy;' align='left' nowrap='true'><a href='" + va[c] + "'>" + va[c] +
"</a></td>\" + vbcrlf)");
    }
    txtstream.WriteLine("</tr>");
}
```

Horizontal Using A ListBox

```
for(var d = 0;d < values.length;d++

{

    txtstream.WriteLine("<tr>");
```

```
        va = values[d];
        for(var c = 0;c < names.length;c++)
        {
            txtstream.WriteLine("<td   style='font-family:Calibri,   Sans-Serif;font-size:
12px;color:navy;' align='left' nowrap='true'><select multiple><option value = '" +
va[c] + "'>" + va[c] + "</option></select></td>\" + vbcrlf)");
        }
        txtstream.WriteLine("</tr>");
    }
```

Horizontal Using A Span

```
    for(var d = 0;d < values.length;d++

    {

        txtstream.WriteLine("<tr>");

        va = values[d];
        for(var c = 0;c < names.length;c++)
        {
            txtstream.WriteLine("<td                    style='color:navy;font-size:10px;font-
family:Cambria, serif;' align='left' nowrap><span>" + va[c] + "</span></td>");
        }
        txtstream.WriteLine("</tr>");
    }
```

Horizontal Using A Textarea

```
    for(var d = 0;d < values.length;d++

    {

        txtstream.WriteLine("<tr>");

        va = values[d];
        for(var c = 0;c < names.length;c++)
        {
```

```
        txtstream.WriteLine("<td                    style='color:navy;font-size:10px;font-
family:Cambria,     serif;'     align='left'    nowrap><textarea>"     +     va[c]    +
"</textarea></td>");
    }
    txtstream.WriteLine("</tr>");
}
```

Horizontal Using A TextBox

```
for(var d = 0;d < values.length;d++

{

    txtstream.WriteLine("<tr>");

    va = values[d];
    for(var c = 0;c < names.length;c++)
    {
        txtstream.WriteLine("<td                    style='color:navy;font-size:10px;font-
family:Cambria, serif;' align='left' nowrap><input Type=text value=\"\" + va[c] +
\"\"></input></td>");

    }
    txtstream.WriteLine("</tr>");
}
```

Vertical No Additional Controls

```
for(var c = 0;c < names.length;c++)
{
    txtstream.WriteLine("<tr><th                style='color:darkred;font-size:10px;font-
family:Cambria, serif;' align='left' nowrap>" + names[c] + "</th>");
    for(var d = 0;d < values.length;d++)
    {
        va = values[d];
        txtstream.WriteLine("<td                    style='color:navy;font-size:10px;font-
family:Cambria, serif;' align='left' nowrap>" + va[c] + "</td>");
    }
```

```
        txtstream.WriteLine("</tr>");
    }
```

Vertical Using A Button

```
    for(var c = 0;c < names.length;c++)
    {
        txtstream.WriteLine("<tr><th          style='color:darkred;font-size:10px;font-
family:Cambria, serif;' align='left' nowrap>" + names[c] + "</th>");
        for(var d = 0;d < values.length;d++)
        {
          va = values[d];
            txtstream.WriteLine("<td              style='color:navy;font-size:10px;font-
family:Cambria, serif;' align='left' nowrap><input Type= button value=\"\" + va[c] +
\"\"></input></td>");
        }
        txtstream.WriteLine("</tr>");
    }
```

Vertical Using A ComboBox

```
    for(var c = 0;c < names.length;c++)
    {
        txtstream.WriteLine("<tr><th          style='color:darkred;font-size:10px;font-
family:Cambria, serif;' align='left' nowrap>" + names[c] + "</th>");
        for(var d = 0;d < values.length;d++)
        {
          va = values[d];
            txtstream.WriteLine("<td    style='font-family:Calibri,   Sans-Serif;font-size:
12px;color:navy;' align='left' nowrap='true'><select><option value = '" + va[c] +
"'>" + va[c] + "</option></select></td>\" + vbcrlf)");
        }
        txtstream.WriteLine("</tr>");
    }
```

Vertical Using A Div

```
for(var c = 0;c < names.length;c++)
{
    txtstream.WriteLine("<tr><th          style='color:darkred;font-size:10px;font-
family:Cambria, serif;' align='left' nowrap>" + names[c] + "</th>");
    for(var d = 0;d < values.length;d++)
    {
      va = values[d];
        txtstream.WriteLine("<td          style='color:navy;font-size:10px;font-
family:Cambria, serif;' align='left' nowrap><div>" + va[c] + "</div></td>");
    }
    txtstream.WriteLine("</tr>")
}
```

Vertical Using A Link

```
for(var c = 0;c < names.length;c++)
{
    txtstream.WriteLine("<tr><th          style='color:darkred;font-size:10px;font-
family:Cambria, serif;' align='left' nowrap>" + names[c] + "</th>");
    for(var d = 0;d < values.length;d++)
    {
      va = values[d];
        txtstream.WriteLine("<td   style='font-family:Calibri,   Sans-Serif;font-size:
12px;color:navy;' align='left' nowrap='true'><a href='" + va[c] + "'>" + va[c] +
"</a></td>\" + vbcrlf)");
    }
    txtstream.WriteLine("</tr>");
}
```

Vertical Using A ListBox

```
for(var c = 0;c < names.length;c++)
{
    txtstream.WriteLine("<tr><th          style='color:darkred;font-size:10px;font-
family:Cambria, serif;' align='left' nowrap>" + names[c] + "</th>");
    for(var d = 0;d < values.length;d++)
    {
      va = values[d];
```

```
        txtstream.WriteLine("<td    style='font-family:Calibri,   Sans-Serif;font-size:
12px;color:navy;' align='left' nowrap='true'><select multiple><option value = '" +
va[c] + "'>" + va[c] + "</option></select></td>\" + vbcrlf)");
    }
    txtstream.WriteLine("</tr>");
  }
```

Vertical Using A Span

```
  for(var c = 0;c < names.length;c++)
  {
      txtstream.WriteLine("<tr><th            style='color:darkred;font-size:10px;font-
family:Cambria, serif;' align='left' nowrap>" + names[c] + "</th>");
      for(var d = 0;d < values.length;d++)
      {
        va = values[d];
        txtstream.WriteLine("<td              style='color:navy;font-size:10px;font-
family:Cambria, serif;' align='left' nowrap><span>" + va[c] + "</span></td>");
      }
      txtstream.WriteLine("</tr>");
  }
```

Vertical Using A Textarea

```
  for(var c = 0;c < names.length;c++)
  {
      txtstream.WriteLine("<tr><th            style='color:darkred;font-size:10px;font-
family:Cambria, serif;' align='left' nowrap>" + names[c] + "</th>");
      for(var d = 0;d < values.length;d++)
      {
        va = values[d];
        txtstream.WriteLine("<td              style='color:navy;font-size:10px;font-
family:Cambria,   serif;'   align='left'   nowrap><textarea>"   +   va[c]   +
"</textarea></td>");
      }
      txtstream.WriteLine("</tr>");
  }
```

Vertical Using A TextBox

```
   for(var c = 0;c < names.length;c++)
   {
       txtstream.WriteLine("<tr><th          style='color:darkred;font-size:10px;font-
family:Cambria, serif;' align='left' nowrap>" + names[c] + "</th>");
      for(var d = 0;d < values.length;d++)
      {
        va = values[d];
        txtstream.WriteLine("<td              style='color:navy;font-size:10px;font-
family:Cambria, serif;' align='left' nowrap><input Type=text value=\"\" + va[c] +
\"\"></input></td>");
      }
      txtstream.WriteLine("</tr>");
   }
```

End Code

```
   txtstream.WriteLine("</table>");
   txtstream.WriteLine("</body>");
   txtstream.WriteLine("</html>");
   txtstream.Close();
}
```

Stylesheets

Decorating your web pages

BELOW ARE SOME STYLESHEETS I COOKED UP THAT I LIKE AND THINK YOU MIGHT TOO. Don't worry I won't be offended if you take and modify to your hearts delight. Please do!

NONE

txtstream.WriteLine('<style type='text/css'>")

txtstream.WriteLine("   th")

txtstream.WriteLine("   begin")

txtstream.WriteLine("   COLOR: darkred;")

txtstream.WriteLine("   BACKGROUND-COLOR: white;")

txtstream.WriteLine("   FONT-FAMILY:font-family: Cambria, serif;")

txtstream.WriteLine("   FONT-SIZE: 12px;")

txtstream.WriteLine("   text-align: left;")

txtstream.WriteLine("   white-Space: nowrap;")

txtstream.WriteLine("   end;")

txtstream.WriteLine("   td")

txtstream.WriteLine("   begin")

txtstream.WriteLine("   COLOR: navy;")

txtstream.WriteLine("   BACKGROUND-COLOR: white;")

```
txtstream.WriteLine("    FONT-FAMILY: font-family: Cambria, serif;")
txtstream.WriteLine("    FONT-SIZE: 12px;")
txtstream.WriteLine("    text-align: left;")
txtstream.WriteLine("    white-Space: nowrap;")
txtstream.WriteLine("    end;")
txtstream.WriteLine("    </style>');
```

BLACK AND WHITE TEXT

```
txtstream.WriteLine("    <style type='text/css'>');
txtstream.WriteLine("    th")
txtstream.WriteLine("    begin")
txtstream.WriteLine("      COLOR: white;")
txtstream.WriteLine("      BACKGROUND-COLOR: black;")
txtstream.WriteLine("      FONT-FAMILY:font-family: Cambria, serif;")
txtstream.WriteLine("      FONT-SIZE: 12px;")
txtstream.WriteLine("      text-align: left;")
txtstream.WriteLine("      white-Space: nowrap;")
txtstream.WriteLine("    end;")
txtstream.WriteLine("    td")
txtstream.WriteLine("    begin")
txtstream.WriteLine("      COLOR: white;")
txtstream.WriteLine("      BACKGROUND-COLOR: black;")
txtstream.WriteLine("      FONT-FAMILY: font-family: Cambria, serif;")
txtstream.WriteLine("      FONT-SIZE: 12px;")
txtstream.WriteLine("      text-align: left;")
```

txtstream.WriteLine(" 	white-Space: nowrap;")

txtstream.WriteLine(" 	end;")

txtstream.WriteLine(" 	div")

txtstream.WriteLine(" 	begin")

txtstream.WriteLine(" 		COLOR: white;")

txtstream.WriteLine(" 		BACKGROUND-COLOR: black;")

txtstream.WriteLine(" 		FONT-FAMILY: font-family: Cambria, serif;")

txtstream.WriteLine(" 		FONT-SIZE: 10px;")

txtstream.WriteLine(" 		text-align: left;")

txtstream.WriteLine(" 		white-Space: nowrap;")

txtstream.WriteLine(" 	end;")

txtstream.WriteLine(" 	span")

txtstream.WriteLine(" 	begin")

txtstream.WriteLine(" 		COLOR: white;")

txtstream.WriteLine(" 		BACKGROUND-COLOR: black;")

txtstream.WriteLine(" 		FONT-FAMILY: font-family: Cambria, serif;")

txtstream.WriteLine(" 		FONT-SIZE: 10px;")

txtstream.WriteLine(" 		text-align: left;")

txtstream.WriteLine(" 		white-Space: nowrap;")

txtstream.WriteLine(" 		display:inline-block;")

txtstream.WriteLine(" 		width: 100%;")

txtstream.WriteLine(" 	end;")

txtstream.WriteLine(" 	textarea")

txtstream.WriteLine(" 	begin")

txtstream.WriteLine(" 		COLOR: white;")

txtstream.WriteLine(" 		BACKGROUND-COLOR: black;")

txtstream.WriteLine(" 		FONT-FAMILY: font-family: Cambria, serif;")

```
txtstream.WriteLine("        FONT-SIZE: 10px;")
txtstream.WriteLine("        text-align: left;")
txtstream.WriteLine("        white-Space: nowrap;")
txtstream.WriteLine("        width: 100%;")
txtstream.WriteLine("    end;")
txtstream.WriteLine("    select")
txtstream.WriteLine("    begin")
txtstream.WriteLine("        COLOR: white;")
txtstream.WriteLine("        BACKGROUND-COLOR: black;")
txtstream.WriteLine("        FONT-FAMILY: font-family: Cambria, serif;")
txtstream.WriteLine("        FONT-SIZE: 10px;")
txtstream.WriteLine("        text-align: left;")
txtstream.WriteLine("        white-Space: nowrap;")
txtstream.WriteLine("        width: 100%;")
txtstream.WriteLine("    end;")
txtstream.WriteLine("    input")
txtstream.WriteLine("    begin")
txtstream.WriteLine("        COLOR: white;")
txtstream.WriteLine("        BACKGROUND-COLOR: black;")
txtstream.WriteLine("        FONT-FAMILY: font-family: Cambria, serif;")
txtstream.WriteLine("        FONT-SIZE: 12px;")
txtstream.WriteLine("        text-align: left;")
txtstream.WriteLine("        display:table-cell;")
txtstream.WriteLine("        white-Space: nowrap;")
txtstream.WriteLine("    end;")
txtstream.WriteLine("    h1 begin")
txtstream.WriteLine("        color: antiquewhite;")
```

txtstream.WriteLine(" text-shadow: 1px 1px 1px black;")

txtstream.WriteLine(" padding: 3px;")

txtstream.WriteLine(" text-align: center;")

txtstream.WriteLine(" box-shadow: inset 2px 2px 5px rgba(0,0,0,0.5);, inset -2px -2px 5px rgba(255,255,255,0.5);;")

txtstream.WriteLine(" end;")

txtstream.WriteLine(" </style>');

COLORED TEXT

txtstream.WriteLine(" <style type='text/css'>');

txtstream.WriteLine(" th")

txtstream.WriteLine(" begin")

txtstream.WriteLine(" COLOR: darkred;")

txtstream.WriteLine(" BACKGROUND-COLOR: #eeeeee;")

txtstream.WriteLine(" FONT-FAMILY:font-family: Cambria, serif;")

txtstream.WriteLine(" FONT-SIZE: 12px;")

txtstream.WriteLine(" text-align: left;")

txtstream.WriteLine(" white-Space: nowrap;")

txtstream.WriteLine(" end;")

txtstream.WriteLine(" td")

txtstream.WriteLine(" begin")

txtstream.WriteLine(" COLOR: navy;")

txtstream.WriteLine(" BACKGROUND-COLOR: #eeeeee;")

txtstream.WriteLine(" FONT-FAMILY: font-family: Cambria, serif;")

txtstream.WriteLine(" FONT-SIZE: 12px;")

txtstream.WriteLine(" text-align: left;")

```
txtstream.WriteLine("    white-Space: nowrap;")
txtstream.WriteLine("   end;")
txtstream.WriteLine("   div")
txtstream.WriteLine("   begin")
txtstream.WriteLine("     COLOR: white;")
txtstream.WriteLine("     BACKGROUND-COLOR: navy;")
txtstream.WriteLine("     FONT-FAMILY: font-family: Cambria, serif;")
txtstream.WriteLine("     FONT-SIZE: 10px;")
txtstream.WriteLine("     text-align: left;")
txtstream.WriteLine("     white-Space: nowrap;")
txtstream.WriteLine("   end;")
txtstream.WriteLine("   span")
txtstream.WriteLine("   begin")
txtstream.WriteLine("     COLOR: white;")
txtstream.WriteLine("     BACKGROUND-COLOR: navy;")
txtstream.WriteLine("     FONT-FAMILY: font-family: Cambria, serif;")
txtstream.WriteLine("     FONT-SIZE: 10px;")
txtstream.WriteLine("     text-align: left;")
txtstream.WriteLine("     white-Space: nowrap;")
txtstream.WriteLine("     display:inline-block;")
txtstream.WriteLine("     width: 100%;")
txtstream.WriteLine("   end;")
txtstream.WriteLine("   textarea")
txtstream.WriteLine("   begin")
txtstream.WriteLine("     COLOR: white;")
txtstream.WriteLine("     BACKGROUND-COLOR: navy;")
txtstream.WriteLine("     FONT-FAMILY: font-family: Cambria, serif;")
```

```
txtstream.WriteLine("      FONT-SIZE: 10px;")
txtstream.WriteLine("      text-align: left;")
txtstream.WriteLine("      white-Space: nowrap;")
txtstream.WriteLine("      width: 100%;")
txtstream.WriteLine("    end;")
txtstream.WriteLine("    select")
txtstream.WriteLine("    begin")
txtstream.WriteLine("      COLOR: white;")
txtstream.WriteLine("      BACKGROUND-COLOR: navy;")
txtstream.WriteLine("      FONT-FAMILY: font-family: Cambria, serif;")
txtstream.WriteLine("      FONT-SIZE: 10px;")
txtstream.WriteLine("      text-align: left;")
txtstream.WriteLine("      white-Space: nowrap;")
txtstream.WriteLine("      width: 100%;")
txtstream.WriteLine("    end;")
txtstream.WriteLine("    input")
txtstream.WriteLine("    begin")
txtstream.WriteLine("      COLOR: white;")
txtstream.WriteLine("      BACKGROUND-COLOR: navy;")
txtstream.WriteLine("      FONT-FAMILY: font-family: Cambria, serif;")
txtstream.WriteLine("      FONT-SIZE: 12px;")
txtstream.WriteLine("      text-align: left;")
txtstream.WriteLine("      display:table-cell;")
txtstream.WriteLine("      white-Space: nowrap;")
txtstream.WriteLine("    end;")
txtstream.WriteLine("    h1 begin")
txtstream.WriteLine("    color: antiquewhite;")
```

```
txtstream.WriteLine("   text-shadow: 1px 1px 1px black;")

txtstream.WriteLine("   padding: 3px;")

txtstream.WriteLine("   text-align: center;")

txtstream.WriteLine("   box-shadow: inset 2px 2px 5px rgba(0,0,0,0.5);, inset -2px
-2px 5px rgba(255,255,255,0.5);;")

txtstream.WriteLine("   end;")

txtstream.WriteLine("   </style>');
```

OSCILLATING ROW COLORS

```
txtstream.WriteLine("   <style>');

txtstream.WriteLine("   th")

txtstream.WriteLine("   begin")

txtstream.WriteLine("      COLOR: white;")

txtstream.WriteLine("      BACKGROUND-COLOR: navy;")

txtstream.WriteLine("      FONT-FAMILY:font-family: Cambria, serif;")

txtstream.WriteLine("      FONT-SIZE: 12px;")

txtstream.WriteLine("      text-align: left;")

txtstream.WriteLine("      white-Space: nowrap;")

txtstream.WriteLine("   end;")

txtstream.WriteLine("   td")

txtstream.WriteLine("   begin")

txtstream.WriteLine("      COLOR: navy;")

txtstream.WriteLine("      FONT-FAMILY: font-family: Cambria, serif;")

txtstream.WriteLine("      FONT-SIZE: 12px;")
```

```
txtstream.WriteLine("    text-align: left;")
txtstream.WriteLine("    white-Space: nowrap;")
txtstream.WriteLine("  end;")
txtstream.WriteLine("  div")
txtstream.WriteLine("  begin")
txtstream.WriteLine("    COLOR: navy;")
txtstream.WriteLine("    FONT-FAMILY: font-family: Cambria, serif;")
txtstream.WriteLine("    FONT-SIZE: 12px;")
txtstream.WriteLine("    text-align: left;")
txtstream.WriteLine("    white-Space: nowrap;")
txtstream.WriteLine("  end;")
txtstream.WriteLine("  span")
txtstream.WriteLine("  begin")
txtstream.WriteLine("    COLOR: navy;")
txtstream.WriteLine("    FONT-FAMILY: font-family: Cambria, serif;")
txtstream.WriteLine("    FONT-SIZE: 12px;")
txtstream.WriteLine("    text-align: left;")
txtstream.WriteLine("    white-Space: nowrap;")
txtstream.WriteLine("    width: 100%;")
txtstream.WriteLine("  end;")
txtstream.WriteLine("  textarea")
txtstream.WriteLine("  begin")
txtstream.WriteLine("    COLOR: navy;")
txtstream.WriteLine("    FONT-FAMILY: font-family: Cambria, serif;")
txtstream.WriteLine("    FONT-SIZE: 12px;")
txtstream.WriteLine("    text-align: left;")
txtstream.WriteLine("    white-Space: nowrap;")
```

```
txtstream.WriteLine("        display:inline-block;")
txtstream.WriteLine("        width: 100%;")
txtstream.WriteLine("    end;")
txtstream.WriteLine("    select")
txtstream.WriteLine("    begin")
txtstream.WriteLine("        COLOR: navy;")
txtstream.WriteLine("        FONT-FAMILY: font-family: Cambria, serif;")
txtstream.WriteLine("        FONT-SIZE: 10px;")
txtstream.WriteLine("        text-align: left;")
txtstream.WriteLine("        white-Space: nowrap;")
txtstream.WriteLine("        display:inline-block;")
txtstream.WriteLine("        width: 100%;")
txtstream.WriteLine("    end;")
txtstream.WriteLine("    input")
txtstream.WriteLine("    begin")
txtstream.WriteLine("        COLOR: navy;")
txtstream.WriteLine("        FONT-FAMILY: font-family: Cambria, serif;")
txtstream.WriteLine("        FONT-SIZE: 12px;")
txtstream.WriteLine("        text-align: left;")
txtstream.WriteLine("        display:table-cell;")
txtstream.WriteLine("        white-Space: nowrap;")
txtstream.WriteLine("    end;")
txtstream.WriteLine("    h1 begin")
txtstream.WriteLine("    color: antiquewhite;")
txtstream.WriteLine("    text-shadow: 1px 1px 1px black;")
txtstream.WriteLine("    padding: 3px;")
txtstream.WriteLine("    text-align: center;")
```

txtstream.WriteLine(" box-shadow: inset 2px 2px 5px rgba(0,0,0,0.5);, inset -2px -2px 5px rgba(255,255,255,0.5);;")

txtstream.WriteLine(" end;")

txtstream.WriteLine(" tr:nth-child(even);beginbackground-color:#f2f2f2;end;")

txtstream.WriteLine(" tr:nth-child(odd);beginbackground-color:#cccccc; color:#f2f2f2;end;")

txtstream.WriteLine(" </style>');

GHOST DECORATED

txtstream.WriteLine(" <style type='text/css'>');

txtstream.WriteLine(" th")

txtstream.WriteLine(" begin")

txtstream.WriteLine(" COLOR: black;")

txtstream.WriteLine(" BACKGROUND-COLOR: white;")

txtstream.WriteLine(" FONT-FAMILY:font-family: Cambria, serif;")

txtstream.WriteLine(" FONT-SIZE: 12px;")

txtstream.WriteLine(" text-align: left;")

txtstream.WriteLine(" white-Space: nowrap;")

txtstream.WriteLine(" end;")

txtstream.WriteLine(" td")

txtstream.WriteLine(" begin")

txtstream.WriteLine(" COLOR: black;")

txtstream.WriteLine(" BACKGROUND-COLOR: white;")

txtstream.WriteLine(" FONT-FAMILY: font-family: Cambria, serif;")

txtstream.WriteLine(" FONT-SIZE: 12px;")

txtstream.WriteLine(" text-align: left;")

txtstream.WriteLine(" white-Space: nowrap;")

txtstream.WriteLine(" end;")

txtstream.WriteLine(" div")

txtstream.WriteLine(" begin")

txtstream.WriteLine("   COLOR: black;")

txtstream.WriteLine("   BACKGROUND-COLOR: white;")

txtstream.WriteLine("   FONT-FAMILY: font-family: Cambria, serif;")

txtstream.WriteLine("   FONT-SIZE: 10px;")

txtstream.WriteLine("   text-align: left;")

txtstream.WriteLine("   white-Space: nowrap;")

txtstream.WriteLine(" end;")

txtstream.WriteLine(" span")

txtstream.WriteLine(" begin")

txtstream.WriteLine("   COLOR: black;")

txtstream.WriteLine("   BACKGROUND-COLOR: white;")

txtstream.WriteLine("   FONT-FAMILY: font-family: Cambria, serif;")

txtstream.WriteLine("   FONT-SIZE: 10px;")

txtstream.WriteLine("   text-align: left;")

txtstream.WriteLine("   white-Space: nowrap;")

txtstream.WriteLine("   display:inline-block;")

txtstream.WriteLine("   width: 100%;")

txtstream.WriteLine(" end;")

txtstream.WriteLine(" textarea")

txtstream.WriteLine(" begin")

txtstream.WriteLine("   COLOR: black;")

txtstream.WriteLine("   BACKGROUND-COLOR: white;")

txtstream.WriteLine("   FONT-FAMILY: font-family: Cambria, serif;")

txtstream.WriteLine("   FONT-SIZE: 10px;")

```
txtstream.WriteLine("      text-align: left;")
txtstream.WriteLine("      white-Space: nowrap;")
txtstream.WriteLine("      width: 100%;")
txtstream.WriteLine("   end;")
txtstream.WriteLine("   select")
txtstream.WriteLine("   begin")
txtstream.WriteLine("      COLOR: black;")
txtstream.WriteLine("      BACKGROUND-COLOR: white;")
txtstream.WriteLine("      FONT-FAMILY: font-family: Cambria, serif;")
txtstream.WriteLine("      FONT-SIZE: 10px;")
txtstream.WriteLine("      text-align: left;")
txtstream.WriteLine("      white-Space: nowrap;")
txtstream.WriteLine("      width: 100%;")
txtstream.WriteLine("   end;")
txtstream.WriteLine("   input")
txtstream.WriteLine("   begin")
txtstream.WriteLine("      COLOR: black;")
txtstream.WriteLine("      BACKGROUND-COLOR: white;")
txtstream.WriteLine("      FONT-FAMILY: font-family: Cambria, serif;")
txtstream.WriteLine("      FONT-SIZE: 12px;")
txtstream.WriteLine("      text-align: left;")
txtstream.WriteLine("      display:table-cell;")
txtstream.WriteLine("      white-Space: nowrap;")
txtstream.WriteLine("   end;")
txtstream.WriteLine("   h1 begin")
txtstream.WriteLine("   color: antiquewhite;")
txtstream.WriteLine("   text-shadow: 1px 1px 1px black;")
```

txtstream.WriteLine(" padding: 3px;")

txtstream.WriteLine(" text-align: center;")

txtstream.WriteLine(" box-shadow: inset 2px 2px 5px rgba(0,0,0,0.5);, inset -2px -2px 5px rgba(255,255,255,0.5);;")

txtstream.WriteLine(" end;")

txtstream.WriteLine(" </style>');

3D

txtstream.WriteLine(" <style type='text/css'>');

txtstream.WriteLine(" body")

txtstream.WriteLine(" begin")

txtstream.WriteLine(" PADDING-RIGHT: 0px;")

txtstream.WriteLine(" PADDING-LEFT: 0px;")

txtstream.WriteLine(" PADDING-BOTTOM: 0px;")

txtstream.WriteLine(" MARGIN: 0px;")

txtstream.WriteLine(" COLOR: #333;")

txtstream.WriteLine(" PADDING-TOP: 0px;")

txtstream.WriteLine(" FONT-FAMILY: verdana, arial, helvetica, sans-serif;")

txtstream.WriteLine(" end;")

txtstream.WriteLine(" table")

txtstream.WriteLine(" begin")

txtstream.WriteLine(" BORDER-RIGHT: #999999 3px solid;")

txtstream.WriteLine(" PADDING-RIGHT: 6px;")

txtstream.WriteLine(" PADDING-LEFT: 6px;")

txtstream.WriteLine(" FONT-WEIGHT: Bold;")

txtstream.WriteLine(" 	FONT-SIZE: 14px;")

txtstream.WriteLine(" 	PADDING-BOTTOM: 6px;")

txtstream.WriteLine(" 	COLOR: Peru;")

txtstream.WriteLine(" 	LINE-HEIGHT: 14px;")

txtstream.WriteLine(" 	PADDING-TOP: 6px;")

txtstream.WriteLine(" 	BORDER-BOTTOM: #999 1px solid;")

txtstream.WriteLine(" 	BACKGROUND-COLOR: #eeeeee;")

txtstream.WriteLine(" 	FONT-FAMILY: verdana, arial, helvetica, sans-serif;")

txtstream.WriteLine(" 	FONT-SIZE: 12px;")

txtstream.WriteLine(" 	end;")

txtstream.WriteLine(" 	th")

txtstream.WriteLine(" 	begin")

txtstream.WriteLine(" 	BORDER-RIGHT: #999999 3px solid;")

txtstream.WriteLine(" 	PADDING-RIGHT: 6px;")

txtstream.WriteLine(" 	PADDING-LEFT: 6px;")

txtstream.WriteLine(" 	FONT-WEIGHT: Bold;")

txtstream.WriteLine(" 	FONT-SIZE: 14px;")

txtstream.WriteLine(" 	PADDING-BOTTOM: 6px;")

txtstream.WriteLine(" 	COLOR: darkred;")

txtstream.WriteLine(" 	LINE-HEIGHT: 14px;")

txtstream.WriteLine(" 	PADDING-TOP: 6px;")

txtstream.WriteLine(" 	BORDER-BOTTOM: #999 1px solid;")

txtstream.WriteLine(" 	BACKGROUND-COLOR: #eeeeee;")

txtstream.WriteLine(" 	FONT-FAMILY:font-family: Cambria, serif;")

txtstream.WriteLine(" 	FONT-SIZE: 12px;")

txtstream.WriteLine(" 	text-align: left;")

txtstream.WriteLine(" 	white-Space: nowrap;")

```
txtstream.WriteLine("   end;")
txtstream.WriteLine("   .th")
txtstream.WriteLine("  begin")
txtstream.WriteLine("      BORDER-RIGHT: #999999 2px solid;")
txtstream.WriteLine("      PADDING-RIGHT: 6px;")
txtstream.WriteLine("      PADDING-LEFT: 6px;")
txtstream.WriteLine("      FONT-WEIGHT: Bold;")
txtstream.WriteLine("      PADDING-BOTTOM: 6px;")
txtstream.WriteLine("      COLOR: black;")
txtstream.WriteLine("      PADDING-TOP: 6px;")
txtstream.WriteLine("      BORDER-BOTTOM: #999 2px solid;")
txtstream.WriteLine("      BACKGROUND-COLOR: #eeeeee;")
txtstream.WriteLine("      FONT-FAMILY: font-family: Cambria, serif;")
txtstream.WriteLine("      FONT-SIZE: 10px;")
txtstream.WriteLine("      text-align: right;")
txtstream.WriteLine("      white-Space: nowrap;")
txtstream.WriteLine("   end;")
txtstream.WriteLine("  td")
txtstream.WriteLine("  begin")
txtstream.WriteLine("      BORDER-RIGHT: #999999 3px solid;")
txtstream.WriteLine("      PADDING-RIGHT: 6px;")
txtstream.WriteLine("      PADDING-LEFT: 6px;")
txtstream.WriteLine("      FONT-WEIGHT: Normal;")
txtstream.WriteLine("      PADDING-BOTTOM: 6px;")
txtstream.WriteLine("      COLOR: navy;")
txtstream.WriteLine("      LINE-HEIGHT: 14px;")
txtstream.WriteLine("      PADDING-TOP: 6px;")
```

```
txtstream.WriteLine("        BORDER-BOTTOM: #999 1px solid;")

txtstream.WriteLine("        BACKGROUND-COLOR: #eeeeee;")

txtstream.WriteLine("        FONT-FAMILY: font-family: Cambria, serif;")

txtstream.WriteLine("        FONT-SIZE: 12px;")

txtstream.WriteLine("        text-align: left;")

txtstream.WriteLine("        white-Space: nowrap;")

txtstream.WriteLine("    end;")

txtstream.WriteLine("    div")

txtstream.WriteLine("    begin")

txtstream.WriteLine("        BORDER-RIGHT: #999999 3px solid;")

txtstream.WriteLine("        PADDING-RIGHT: 6px;")

txtstream.WriteLine("        PADDING-LEFT: 6px;")

txtstream.WriteLine("        FONT-WEIGHT: Normal;")

txtstream.WriteLine("        PADDING-BOTTOM: 6px;")

txtstream.WriteLine("        COLOR: white;")

txtstream.WriteLine("        PADDING-TOP: 6px;")

txtstream.WriteLine("        BORDER-BOTTOM: #999 1px solid;")

txtstream.WriteLine("        BACKGROUND-COLOR: navy;")

txtstream.WriteLine("        FONT-FAMILY: font-family: Cambria, serif;")

txtstream.WriteLine("        FONT-SIZE: 10px;")

txtstream.WriteLine("        text-align: left;")

txtstream.WriteLine("        white-Space: nowrap;")

txtstream.WriteLine("    end;")

txtstream.WriteLine("    span")

txtstream.WriteLine("    begin")

txtstream.WriteLine("        BORDER-RIGHT: #999999 3px solid;")

txtstream.WriteLine("        PADDING-RIGHT: 3px;")
```

```
txtstream.WriteLine("        PADDING-LEFT: 3px;")

txtstream.WriteLine("        FONT-WEIGHT: Normal;")

txtstream.WriteLine("        PADDING-BOTTOM: 3px;")

txtstream.WriteLine("        COLOR: white;")

txtstream.WriteLine("        PADDING-TOP: 3px;")

txtstream.WriteLine("        BORDER-BOTTOM: #999 1px solid;")

txtstream.WriteLine("        BACKGROUND-COLOR: navy;")

txtstream.WriteLine("        FONT-FAMILY: font-family: Cambria, serif;")

txtstream.WriteLine("        FONT-SIZE: 10px;")

txtstream.WriteLine("        text-align: left;")

txtstream.WriteLine("        white-Space: nowrap;")

txtstream.WriteLine("        display:inline-block;")

txtstream.WriteLine("        width: 100%;")

txtstream.WriteLine("    end;")

txtstream.WriteLine("    textarea")

txtstream.WriteLine("    begin")

txtstream.WriteLine("        BORDER-RIGHT: #999999 3px solid;")

txtstream.WriteLine("        PADDING-RIGHT: 3px;")

txtstream.WriteLine("        PADDING-LEFT: 3px;")

txtstream.WriteLine("        FONT-WEIGHT: Normal;")

txtstream.WriteLine("        PADDING-BOTTOM: 3px;")

txtstream.WriteLine("        COLOR: white;")

txtstream.WriteLine("        PADDING-TOP: 3px;")

txtstream.WriteLine("        BORDER-BOTTOM: #999 1px solid;")

txtstream.WriteLine("        BACKGROUND-COLOR: navy;")

txtstream.WriteLine("        FONT-FAMILY: font-family: Cambria, serif;")

txtstream.WriteLine("        FONT-SIZE: 10px;")
```

```
txtstream.WriteLine("        text-align: left;")
txtstream.WriteLine("        white-Space: nowrap;")
txtstream.WriteLine("        width: 100%;")
txtstream.WriteLine("     end;")
txtstream.WriteLine("    select")
txtstream.WriteLine("    begin")
txtstream.WriteLine("        BORDER-RIGHT: #999999 3px solid;")
txtstream.WriteLine("        PADDING-RIGHT: 6px;")
txtstream.WriteLine("        PADDING-LEFT: 6px;")
txtstream.WriteLine("        FONT-WEIGHT: Normal;")
txtstream.WriteLine("        PADDING-BOTTOM: 6px;")
txtstream.WriteLine("        COLOR: white;")
txtstream.WriteLine("        PADDING-TOP: 6px;")
txtstream.WriteLine("        BORDER-BOTTOM: #999 1px solid;")
txtstream.WriteLine("        BACKGROUND-COLOR: navy;")
txtstream.WriteLine("        FONT-FAMILY: font-family: Cambria, serif;")
txtstream.WriteLine("        FONT-SIZE: 10px;")
txtstream.WriteLine("        text-align: left;")
txtstream.WriteLine("        white-Space: nowrap;")
txtstream.WriteLine("        width: 100%;")
txtstream.WriteLine("     end;")
txtstream.WriteLine("    input")
txtstream.WriteLine("    begin")
txtstream.WriteLine("        BORDER-RIGHT: #999999 3px solid;")
txtstream.WriteLine("        PADDING-RIGHT: 3px;")
txtstream.WriteLine("        PADDING-LEFT: 3px;")
txtstream.WriteLine("        FONT-WEIGHT: Bold;")
```

```
txtstream.WriteLine("          PADDING-BOTTOM: 3px;")

txtstream.WriteLine("          COLOR: white;")

txtstream.WriteLine("          PADDING-TOP: 3px;")

txtstream.WriteLine("          BORDER-BOTTOM: #999 1px solid;")

txtstream.WriteLine("          BACKGROUND-COLOR: navy;")

txtstream.WriteLine("          FONT-FAMILY: font-family: Cambria, serif;")

txtstream.WriteLine("          FONT-SIZE: 12px;")

txtstream.WriteLine("          text-align: left;")

txtstream.WriteLine("          display:table-cell;")

txtstream.WriteLine("          white-Space: nowrap;")

txtstream.WriteLine("          width: 100%;")

txtstream.WriteLine("    end;")

txtstream.WriteLine("    h1 begin")

txtstream.WriteLine("    color: antiquewhite;")

txtstream.WriteLine("    text-shadow: 1px 1px 1px black;")

txtstream.WriteLine("    padding: 3px;")

txtstream.WriteLine("    text-align: center;")

txtstream.WriteLine("    box-shadow: inset 2px 2px 5px rgba(0,0,0,0.5);, inset -2px -2px 5px rgba(255,255,255,0.5);;")

txtstream.WriteLine("    end;")

txtstream.WriteLine("    </style>');
```

SHADOW BOX

```
txtstream.WriteLine("    <style type='text/css'>');

txtstream.WriteLine("    body")

txtstream.WriteLine("    begin")
```

txtstream.WriteLine("   PADDING-RIGHT: 0px;")

txtstream.WriteLine("   PADDING-LEFT: 0px;")

txtstream.WriteLine("   PADDING-BOTTOM: 0px;")

txtstream.WriteLine("   MARGIN: 0px;")

txtstream.WriteLine("   COLOR: #333;")

txtstream.WriteLine("   PADDING-TOP: 0px;")

txtstream.WriteLine("   FONT-FAMILY: verdana, arial, helvetica, sans-serif;")

txtstream.WriteLine("   end;")

txtstream.WriteLine("   table")

txtstream.WriteLine("   begin")

txtstream.WriteLine("   BORDER-RIGHT: #999999 1px solid;")

txtstream.WriteLine("   PADDING-RIGHT: 1px;")

txtstream.WriteLine("   PADDING-LEFT: 1px;")

txtstream.WriteLine("   PADDING-BOTTOM: 1px;")

txtstream.WriteLine("   LINE-HEIGHT: 8px;")

txtstream.WriteLine("   PADDING-TOP: 1px;")

txtstream.WriteLine("   BORDER-BOTTOM: #999 1px solid;")

txtstream.WriteLine("   BACKGROUND-COLOR: #eeeeee;")

txtstream.WriteLine(" filter:progid:DXImageTransform.Microsoft.Shadow(color='silver', Direction=135, Strength=16")

txtstream.WriteLine("   end;")

txtstream.WriteLine("   th")

txtstream.WriteLine("   begin")

txtstream.WriteLine("   BORDER-RIGHT: #999999 3px solid;")

txtstream.WriteLine("   PADDING-RIGHT: 6px;")

txtstream.WriteLine("   PADDING-LEFT: 6px;")

txtstream.WriteLine("   FONT-WEIGHT: Bold;")

```
txtstream.WriteLine("        FONT-SIZE: 14px;")

txtstream.WriteLine("        PADDING-BOTTOM: 6px;")

txtstream.WriteLine("        COLOR: darkred;")

txtstream.WriteLine("        LINE-HEIGHT: 14px;")

txtstream.WriteLine("        PADDING-TOP: 6px;")

txtstream.WriteLine("        BORDER-BOTTOM: #999 1px solid;")

txtstream.WriteLine("        BACKGROUND-COLOR: #eeeeee;")

txtstream.WriteLine("        FONT-FAMILY: font-family: Cambria, serif;")

txtstream.WriteLine("        FONT-SIZE: 12px;")

txtstream.WriteLine("        text-align: left;")

txtstream.WriteLine("        white-Space: nowrap;")

txtstream.WriteLine("    end;")

txtstream.WriteLine("    .th")

txtstream.WriteLine("    begin")

txtstream.WriteLine("        BORDER-RIGHT: #999999 2px solid;")

txtstream.WriteLine("        PADDING-RIGHT: 6px;")

txtstream.WriteLine("        PADDING-LEFT: 6px;")

txtstream.WriteLine("        FONT-WEIGHT: Bold;")

txtstream.WriteLine("        PADDING-BOTTOM: 6px;")

txtstream.WriteLine("        COLOR: black;")

txtstream.WriteLine("        PADDING-TOP: 6px;")

txtstream.WriteLine("        BORDER-BOTTOM: #999 2px solid;")

txtstream.WriteLine("        BACKGROUND-COLOR: #eeeeee;")

txtstream.WriteLine("        FONT-FAMILY: font-family: Cambria, serif;")

txtstream.WriteLine("        FONT-SIZE: 10px;")

txtstream.WriteLine("        text-align: right;")

txtstream.WriteLine("        white-Space: nowrap;")
```

```
txtstream.WriteLine("    end;")

txtstream.WriteLine("    td")

txtstream.WriteLine("    begin")

txtstream.WriteLine("        BORDER-RIGHT: #999999 3px solid;")

txtstream.WriteLine("        PADDING-RIGHT: 6px;")

txtstream.WriteLine("        PADDING-LEFT: 6px;")

txtstream.WriteLine("        FONT-WEIGHT: Normal;")

txtstream.WriteLine("        PADDING-BOTTOM: 6px;")

txtstream.WriteLine("        COLOR: navy;")

txtstream.WriteLine("        LINE-HEIGHT: 14px;")

txtstream.WriteLine("        PADDING-TOP: 6px;")

txtstream.WriteLine("        BORDER-BOTTOM: #999 1px solid;")

txtstream.WriteLine("        BACKGROUND-COLOR: #eeeeee;")

txtstream.WriteLine("        FONT-FAMILY: font-family: Cambria, serif;")

txtstream.WriteLine("        FONT-SIZE: 12px;")

txtstream.WriteLine("        text-align: left;")

txtstream.WriteLine("        white-Space: nowrap;")

txtstream.WriteLine("    end;")

txtstream.WriteLine("    div")

txtstream.WriteLine("    begin")

txtstream.WriteLine("        BORDER-RIGHT: #999999 3px solid;")

txtstream.WriteLine("        PADDING-RIGHT: 6px;")

txtstream.WriteLine("        PADDING-LEFT: 6px;")

txtstream.WriteLine("        FONT-WEIGHT: Normal;")

txtstream.WriteLine("        PADDING-BOTTOM: 6px;")

txtstream.WriteLine("        COLOR: white;")

txtstream.WriteLine("        PADDING-TOP: 6px;")
```

```
txtstream.WriteLine("          BORDER-BOTTOM: #999 1px solid;")
txtstream.WriteLine("          BACKGROUND-COLOR: navy;")
txtstream.WriteLine("          FONT-FAMILY: font-family: Cambria, serif;")
txtstream.WriteLine("          FONT-SIZE: 10px;")
txtstream.WriteLine("          text-align: left;")
txtstream.WriteLine("          white-Space: nowrap;")
txtstream.WriteLine("     end;")
txtstream.WriteLine("     span")
txtstream.WriteLine("     begin")
txtstream.WriteLine("          BORDER-RIGHT: #999999 3px solid;")
txtstream.WriteLine("          PADDING-RIGHT: 3px;")
txtstream.WriteLine("          PADDING-LEFT: 3px;")
txtstream.WriteLine("          FONT-WEIGHT: Normal;")
txtstream.WriteLine("          PADDING-BOTTOM: 3px;")
txtstream.WriteLine("          COLOR: white;")
txtstream.WriteLine("          PADDING-TOP: 3px;")
txtstream.WriteLine("          BORDER-BOTTOM: #999 1px solid;")
txtstream.WriteLine("          BACKGROUND-COLOR: navy;")
txtstream.WriteLine("          FONT-FAMILY: font-family: Cambria, serif;")
txtstream.WriteLine("          FONT-SIZE: 10px;")
txtstream.WriteLine("          text-align: left;")
txtstream.WriteLine("          white-Space: nowrap;")
txtstream.WriteLine("          display: inline-block;")
txtstream.WriteLine("          width: 100%;")
txtstream.WriteLine("     end;")
txtstream.WriteLine("     textarea")
txtstream.WriteLine("     begin")
```

```
txtstream.WriteLine("        BORDER-RIGHT: #999999 3px solid;")

txtstream.WriteLine("        PADDING-RIGHT: 3px;")

txtstream.WriteLine("        PADDING-LEFT: 3px;")

txtstream.WriteLine("        FONT-WEIGHT: Normal;")

txtstream.WriteLine("        PADDING-BOTTOM: 3px;")

txtstream.WriteLine("        COLOR: white;")

txtstream.WriteLine("        PADDING-TOP: 3px;")

txtstream.WriteLine("        BORDER-BOTTOM: #999 1px solid;")

txtstream.WriteLine("        BACKGROUND-COLOR: navy;")

txtstream.WriteLine("        FONT-FAMILY: font-family: Cambria, serif;")

txtstream.WriteLine("        FONT-SIZE: 10px;")

txtstream.WriteLine("        text-align: left;")

txtstream.WriteLine("        white-Space: nowrap;")

txtstream.WriteLine("        width: 100%;")

txtstream.WriteLine("    end;")

txtstream.WriteLine("    select")

txtstream.WriteLine("    begin")

txtstream.WriteLine("        BORDER-RIGHT: #999999 3px solid;")

txtstream.WriteLine("        PADDING-RIGHT: 6px;")

txtstream.WriteLine("        PADDING-LEFT: 6px;")

txtstream.WriteLine("        FONT-WEIGHT: Normal;")

txtstream.WriteLine("        PADDING-BOTTOM: 6px;")

txtstream.WriteLine("        COLOR: white;")

txtstream.WriteLine("        PADDING-TOP: 6px;")

txtstream.WriteLine("        BORDER-BOTTOM: #999 1px solid;")

txtstream.WriteLine("        BACKGROUND-COLOR: navy;")

txtstream.WriteLine("        FONT-FAMILY: font-family: Cambria, serif;")
```

```
txtstream.WriteLine("        FONT-SIZE: 10px;")

txtstream.WriteLine("        text-align: left;")

txtstream.WriteLine("        white-Space: nowrap;")

txtstream.WriteLine("        width: 100%;")

txtstream.WriteLine("    end;")

txtstream.WriteLine("    input")

txtstream.WriteLine("    begin")

txtstream.WriteLine("        BORDER-RIGHT: #999999 3px solid;")

txtstream.WriteLine("        PADDING-RIGHT: 3px;")

txtstream.WriteLine("        PADDING-LEFT: 3px;")

txtstream.WriteLine("        FONT-WEIGHT: Bold;")

txtstream.WriteLine("        PADDING-BOTTOM: 3px;")

txtstream.WriteLine("        COLOR: white;")

txtstream.WriteLine("        PADDING-TOP: 3px;")

txtstream.WriteLine("        BORDER-BOTTOM: #999 1px solid;")

txtstream.WriteLine("        BACKGROUND-COLOR: navy;")

txtstream.WriteLine("        FONT-FAMILY: font-family: Cambria, serif;")

txtstream.WriteLine("        FONT-SIZE: 12px;")

txtstream.WriteLine("        text-align: left;")

txtstream.WriteLine("        display: table-cell;")

txtstream.WriteLine("        white-Space: nowrap;")

txtstream.WriteLine("        width: 100%;")

txtstream.WriteLine("    end;")

txtstream.WriteLine("    h1 begin")

txtstream.WriteLine("    color: antiquewhite;")

txtstream.WriteLine("    text-shadow: 1px 1px 1px black;")

txtstream.WriteLine("    padding: 3px;")
```

txtstream.WriteLine(" text-align: center;")

txtstream.WriteLine(" box-shadow: inset 2px 2px 5px rgba(0,0,0,0.5);, inset -2px -2px 5px rgba(255,255,255,0.5);;")

txtstream.WriteLine(" end;")

txtstream.WriteLine(" </style>');

www.ingramcontent.com/pod-product-compliance
Lightning Source LLC
Chambersburg PA
CBHW070842070326
40690CB00009B/1663